BUILDING INDESTRUCTIBLE SELF-CONFIDENCE FOR TEENS

A GUIDE TO FIND UNIQUE INNER STRENGTHS, BOOST SELF-ESTEEM, CONQUER FEAR OF WHAT OTHERS THINK & OVERCOME INSECURITIES TO EMBRACE YOUR TRUE SELF

JAMIE FRAZIER

© Copyright Jamie Frazier 2023 - All rights reserved.

The content contained within this book may not be reproduced, duplicated, or transmitted without direct written permission from the author or the publisher.

Under no circumstances will any blame or legal responsibility be held against the publisher, or author, for any damages, reparation, or monetary loss due to the information contained within this book, either directly or indirectly.

Legal Notice:

This book is copyright protected. It is only for personal use. You cannot amend, distribute, sell, use, quote, or paraphrase any part, or the content within this book, without the author or publisher's permission.

Disclaimer Notice:

Please note that the information contained within this document is for educational and entertainment purposes only. All effort has been executed to present accurate, up-to-date, reliable, complete information. No warranties of any kind are declared or implied. Readers acknowledge that the author is not rendering legal, financial, medical, or professional advice. The content within this book has been derived from various sources. Please consult a licensed professional before attempting any techniques outlined in this book.

By reading this document, the reader agrees that under no circumstances is the author responsible for any losses, direct or indirect, that are incurred due to the use of the information in this document, including, but not limited to, errors, omissions, or inaccuracies.

CONTENTS

Introduction   7

1. UNDERSTANDING YOUR STRUGGLES   15
   Understanding Self-confidence and Self-esteem   17
   Top Reasons Why People Experience Low Self-Confidence   19
   Top Reasons for Low Self-Esteem   22
   Signs of Low Self-Confidence and Self-Esteem   25

2. BUILDING BLOCKS OF CONFIDENCE   31
   Do's & Don'ts For Self-Confidence   33
   Regain Your Confidence   36
   Keeping Good Company   41
   Social Anxiety   46

3. THE GUILT POISON   55
   Types Of Guilt   59
   Is Guilt Good?   62
   Guilt And Overthinking   64
   Guilt-Free   65
   Think About It   71

4. THE SCIENCE OF EMOTIONS   73
   Basics Of Emotions   75
   Types Of Emotions   78
   Emotions and Thoughts   83
   Negative Emotions   84
   Identify Negative Emotions   87
   Self-confidence and Emotions   90
   How To Control Your Emotions   91

5. TEENAGE AFFECTION FOR SOCIAL
   MEDIA 97
   The Web Of Social Media 99
   Impact of Social Media 101
   How Can Parents Help? 106

6. ELIMINATING PROCRASTINATION 111
   What is Procrastination? 112
   The Link Between Self-Confidence and
   Procrastination 114
   Types of Procrastinators 116
   Overthinker meets the Procrastinator ... 117
   How to overcome procrastination 118

7. BUILDING YOURSELF UP 121
   The Basics Of Self-Care 122
   Strategies To Improve Self-Care 129
   Acceptance and Love 130

8. MINDING YOUR THOUGHTS 135
   Causes of Negative Self Talk 137
   Consequences of Negative Self Talk 140
   Types of Negative Self-Talk 143
   Silence The Critic 145
   Shifting The Energies 148
   Rebuild Your Confidence 151
   Positive Affirmations 155

9. BUILDING YOURSELF FROM WITHIN .. 159
   Overview Of Inner Strength 161
   Growth Mindset 164

10. BREAKING A SWEAT 169
    Benefits of Exercise 170
    Workout Timeline 174
    Meditation 175

11. UNLOCKING THE POWER OF WORDS 183
Importance of Journalism 184
Benefits of journaling 185
How to journal 187
Journaling and Self Confidence 188
Self-Love Journal Prompts 189

Conclusion 193
References 199

INTRODUCTION

"With the realization of one's own potential and self-confidence in one's own ability, one can build a better world"

— DALAI LAMA

Teenage years can be some of the most challenging times in a person's life. It is common for teenagers to suffer from depression, anxiety, and distress during these years. Anxiety, self-doubt, and stress are all a byproduct of low self-confidence. Teenage years are crucial for personal growth, but depression and anxiety can devastate a young person's life, leading to concerns over academic performance, social relationships, and physical health. Have you ever felt like the weight of the world is too much?

As a lack of self-confidence conquers your mind and overthinking plagues your intrusive thoughts, you would think that your fate is sealed. It's not. This is not a never-ending doom. Instead, it is just a difficult time in your life that will pass. Please do not abandon yourself, especially not in the name of trying to be seen, heard, and validated by temporary connections.

Stop holding onto things that do not demonstrate respect for your value. You deserve so much more. We often wait for happy endings but forget we possess the power to create those endings.

Did you know that the Titanic & Mare of Eastown star Kate Winslet was bullied throughout high school for being overweight? So much so that her theater teacher suggested that she should do something else, imagine being told to divert yourself towards different interests merely because you do not fit the role of an actress.

Do you know what Kate did? The exact opposite, of course! Her secret lies within her confidence, and look where she is now! Her face is plastered through billboards all around the world, and with an Oscar, an Emmy, and several other awards to her name, she shows no intention of slowing down. She created her happy ending because she took back control from the adversaries of life and refused to kneel in front of those who did not believe in her.

Every person you encounter in your life is fighting a battle of their own. It is often quietly done with no collateral damage, but it's essential to understand that you are not alone. Whether you suffer from childhood trauma or emotional abuse, it all adds up to low self-confidence. Suppose you find yourself replaying hurtful memories from your childhood. In that case, it is possible that the childhood trauma you incurred from specific life experiences adversely affects your mental health.

Sadly, the numbers increase for teens struggling with a lack of confidence. According to a study conducted by Quenqua, it was identified that more than 40% of middle and high school boys regularly exercise to increase muscle mass (Quenqua, 2012). I call this the Efron effect, where young boys are forced to gain muscle to look remotely attractive in their circles. However, this body dysphoria only adds more fuel to the fire of depression. There is nothing wrong with wanting to look and feel good with a healthy exercise routine. However, there comes pressure with keeping up appearances when you feel you have to go to the gym to look a certain way.

While filming his hit movie, High School Musical, Zac Efron was only 18 when he was forced to lose several pounds and bulk his growing body with muscles. Something that you now frequently see teenagers do. As the years passed by, Efron became insecure about his body. Until recently, he opened up about his struggle with body image and how he is giving himself time to heal. Did you know that boys stop growing by 18 and girls stop growing after puberty which varies between the age of 16-18? In a study done by Karimian, it was stated that the maximum growing age for boys is 22. Imagine constantly criticizing your growing body. It's still changing, and it's beautiful.

It is important to be kind to yourself. As your body grows, so does your mind. Eventually, you will see that life is full of unpredictability. The constant thoughts that plague your mind about how others perceive and value you. It gets so much that you automatically try to find ways that can save relationships from getting destroyed often leads to people pleasing. You feel entangled in the quest to become like somebody else to grab attention or please others, and you forget that you are unique in your own wonderful way.

It happens to everyone. As you grow up, the world and life surprise you. You find out who you are and what you want, and then you realize that people you have known forever don't see things from the same lens. So, you keep beautiful memories but find yourself moving on because life does not stop for anyone. Confidence is able to keep you afloat when the treacheries of life thrust you into a high tide.

For many people, social media is a part of their everyday life. Some use it for their business, while others use it as an inspiration. However, a small part looms with darkness and constantly impacts women. In particular teenage girls have shown larger signs of depression due to online bullying. In fact, girls aged 11-14 have reported feeling unhappy with their bodies and appearance (Broster, 2021). Have you ever found yourself in a quarrel with someone on social media?

While social media is a place of great networking, it adversely affects impressionable minds. These girls are engulfed in negative self-talk and focus on their flaws instead of their qualities and achievements. When anything goes wrong, they start finding faults in themselves, whether their personality, appearance, behavior, or abilities. It wastes their potential and reduces them to the desire to look and feel a way that might be fake.

That said, teenage years are the hardest times for young people. As a 20-year-old, I was always keen on learning everything about teenage mental health, mainly because I felt the pain personally. So what brought me to this point? To tell you a bit about me. Life was hard for me as a teenager. I came to learn at the age of 13 that my mother suffered severely from Alcoholism. My whole life up to that point, I had no idea about her illness as she was sober during my childhood. My parents split when I was five years old. I would visit my Dad mainly on weekends, so she was my primary carer then. My father really steadied the ship during this time. He helped me get through school, taught me many great lessons about focusing and loving yourself through times when the people closest to you are suffering, and we built a great relationship that we didn't previously have. My mother's sobriety was very on and off at that time and still is to this day. Over time, I've learned to cope with it due to my father's guidance, but I struggled initially. It was very emotional building the relationship back up with her after being through treatment and thinking she was on the other side. Suddenly, a relapse would happen, and she would have to go away for 12 weeks again.

So what effect did all of this have? In school, I was extremely emotionally unstable, lacking confidence, and felt isolated walking the corridors, knowing nobody knows what I'm going through. I would be very awkward and uncomfortable in social settings, particularly at parties. In these settings, I would cry a lot and get upset. Nobody knew why. Even if I tried to explain it to close friends, it was still a lot for them to understand, which made it even more isolating for me. I was bullied for a while, and people would sing Bob Marley's song 'no woman, no cry' to me. It doesn't make much sense, but I knew exactly what their sniggering meant.

It got to the point where I got into a petty school fight with the main perpetrator of the bullying. I stood up for myself and got the better of him, and he never bothered me again after that. We ended up being very good friends. I do not condone violence of any sort, but there is undoubtedly a lot of merit in standing up to your bullies.

I love my mother dearly, and we are the best of friends. However, when she has stages where she relapses, I have learned over time, with the help of my father, how to deal with it by completely removing myself from the situation and focusing on myself. From my studies, sports, work life, and other relationships. It took time, experience, and practice to deal with it, and it ultimately made me very self-aware, rational, and wiser in coping with stressful situations.

There's a bit about my story. Some aspects may resonate with what you are going through, and my story is my motivation for writing Building Indestructible Self-Confidence for Teens. The book is a reflection of my experiences. I curated this especially to help teenagers calm their inner critic and boost their self-confidence. The main idea behind it is to equip yourself with the essential tools of confidence that you can use to help yourself and others. Confidence allows you to take healthy risks, try out new things and solve problems creatively. This book is the ultimate solution for stopping feeling inadequate and unloved and focusing on building your self-confidence and polishing your distinctive personality without worrying about pleasing others. You will explore different tools, such as building blocks of confidence and how to eliminate guilt from your life. So, without further ado, let's get into it!

1

UNDERSTANDING YOUR STRUGGLES

"Self-esteem comes from who you have in your life. How you were raised. What you struggled with as a child."

— HALLE BERRY

As I walked into the bustling coffee shop, I couldn't help but notice the woman sitting in the corner. She seemed familiar, and with a jolt, I realized it was none other than Sasha, an old schoolmate of mine. She was hunched over her laptop, her eyes darting back and forth as she furiously typed away. However, the way she carried herself caught my attention the most. Despite her intense focus, there was a certain air of confidence and self-assuredness about her that was hard to ignore. One could feel the strength of her confidence, and how she carries herself, it's always refreshing to meet her.

As I ordered my coffee, I couldn't help but wonder what it was about this woman that made her so confident. Was it her job? Her upbringing? Or was it something else entirely? Because I remembered her from middle school, but somewhat differently.

It was hard to believe that the same girl who appeared confident now had her fair share of insecurities. At a young age, Sasha's home life became unpleasant due to her parents' frequent arguments. Her sensitivity and anxiety made her believe she was at fault for the conflicts. The prolonged exposure to family conflicts damaged Sasha's self-esteem, making it challenging for her to form friendships at middle school. She constantly remained concerned about others' perceptions and values, wondering if she did something to make her friends dislike her. Despite being an empathetic and funny person, Sasha feared connecting with others.

In today's society, self-confidence plays a crucial role in one's personal and professional success. Have you ever found yourself hesitating to speak up in a discussion session or doubting your abilities before a presentation in front of your teacher? We've all experienced moments of self-doubt, but what about those who constantly struggle with low self-confidence?

It can affect everything from how we communicate with others to the opportunities we pursue. However, it's not uncommon for life experiences and external factors to knock us down and leave us feeling unsure of ourselves.

But fear not! There are ways to boost our confidence and regain our sense of self-worth. In this book, we'll explore the nature of self-confidence, its causes, and its effects on our lives. We'll also delve into practical techniques for restoring and maintaining self-confidence so that you can conquer any challenge that comes your way. So if you're ready to break free from self-doubt and become your most confident self, let's dive in!

UNDERSTANDING SELF-CONFIDENCE AND SELF-ESTEEM

When it comes to building a strong sense of self, self-confidence and self-esteem, play a vital role.

Are you struggling with low self-confidence or self-esteem? Don't worry; you are not alone. Many people face similar issues, especially teenagers. However, understanding the difference between the two concepts and their root causes can help you overcome these challenges.

Let's begin by defining self-confidence and self-esteem. According to Healthline, self-confidence is "the belief in your abilities and qualities," while self-esteem is "the overall sense of self-worth and value" that you hold. These two concepts are closely related, but they are distinct. Self-confidence is more focused on your belief in your abilities, while self-esteem is more focused on your overall sense of worth.

Now, why are self-confidence and self-esteem so important?

For starters, self-confidence allows you to take on new challenges and push yourself out of your comfort zone. It helps you trust in your abilities and make decisions with conviction. Self-confidence can also help you develop better relationships, both personal and professional, by allowing you to communicate more effectively and assertively.

On the other hand, self-esteem is crucial for your mental health and well-being. When you have a positive sense of self-worth, you're more likely to have a positive outlook on life and feel better about yourself. This, in turn, can help reduce stress and anxiety, improve your relationships, and lead to a more fulfilling life.

But what if you're struggling with low self-confidence or self-esteem?

According to Psychology Today, there are various reasons why this might be the case. Some factors contributing to low self-confidence and self-esteem include genetics, temperament, life experiences, misinformation, unsupportive environments, and mental health conditions like anxiety and depression.

Have you ever felt your lack of confidence is holding you back from achieving your goals?

Do you find yourself constantly doubting your abilities or comparing yourself to others?

TOP REASONS WHY PEOPLE EXPERIENCE LOW SELF-CONFIDENCE

As human beings, it's normal to experience moments of self-doubt and insecurity. However, for some people, these feelings can be pervasive and significantly impact their lives. Low self-confidence can affect people of all ages, but it is widespread among teenagers. According to a resource from Raising Children Network, a website supported by the Australian government, self-esteem and confidence levels in teenagers can be impacted by a variety of factors.

Here are some of the top reasons why people, especially teens, experience low self-confidence:

1. Genes and temperament

While some people are naturally more confident than others, research has shown that genetics play a role in self-confidence levels. Some individuals are simply born with a predisposition towards lower self-esteem and confidence levels. This can be due to their genetic makeup or their temperament. But that's not to say this cannot be solved.

2. Life experiences

Life experiences, particularly during childhood and adolescence, can significantly impact self-confidence. Negative experiences, such as bullying or abuse, can cause individuals to doubt themselves and their abilities. My experiences with my mother's illness were my main source of lacking confidence as a teenager. On the other hand, positive experiences, such as encouragement and support from parents or teachers, can help boost self-confidence.

Have you ever experienced a traumatic or negative event that has affected your self-confidence?

3. Misinformation

Misinformation can be a significant factor in low self-confidence. For example, unrealistic beauty standards portrayed in the media can cause individuals to feel insecure about their appearance. Similarly, incorrect information about abilities or intelligence can lead to feelings of inadequacy.

4. The surroundings

The people and environment we surround ourselves with can significantly impact our self-confidence levels. Negative or unsupportive individuals can bring us down and make us feel inadequate, while positive and supportive individuals can help build us up and increase our confidence. You may feel like best friends and close family members.

Have you ever been in an environment that brought you down and made you feel less confident? You may feel like best friends, and close family members are not good for you to be around constantly, although they give you joy and make you laugh from time to time. It's important to set boundaries with these people, not to necessarily remove them from your life.

5. Anxiety and depression

Anxiety and depression can have a significant impact on self-confidence levels. These mental health conditions can cause individuals to doubt their abilities and worth, leading to feelings of low self-esteem and confidence.

According to a resource from ReachOut, a mental health organization, teenagers with low self-esteem and confidence are more likely to experience symptoms of depression and anxiety. In addition, low self-esteem can also lead to academic underachievement, social withdrawal, and risky behavior. It's important to note that low self-confidence is a common issue that many people face, and it's okay to ask for help. Seeking support from a mental health professional can help identify and address the underlying issues.

TOP REASONS FOR LOW SELF-ESTEEM

Various factors can cause low self-esteem, and understanding these underlying causes can help identify and address the issue.

1. Chronic abuse and criticism

People who have experienced persistent criticism or abuse, whether physical, emotional, or verbal, are more likely to develop low self-esteem. Repeated negative feedback from others can lead individuals to internalize these messages and believe that they are unworthy or incompetent. According to a study published in the Journal of Psychiatric Research, individuals who reported higher levels of childhood abuse had lower levels of self-esteem in adulthood.

2. Adverse Childhood Experiences (ACEs)

ACEs are another significant factor that can cause low self-esteem. ACEs such as neglect, abuse, or growing up in a dysfunctional household can significantly impact a person's self-esteem. These experiences can make it challenging for children to develop a positive sense of self-worth, leading to negative self-talk and feelings of inadequacy. In fact, according to a study published in the journal Pediatrics, children who experience ACEs are at a higher risk of developing low self-esteem, which can have a long-lasting impact on their mental health and well-being.

3. Social Pressures and Expectations

Social expectations, such as those related to beauty standards or academic achievement, can contribute to feelings of low self-esteem. Comparison with others and a fear of not measuring up can make individuals feel inadequate and unworthy. According to a survey conducted by the American Psychological Association, 44% of women and 31% of men report feeling pressure to conform to specific beauty standards.

4. Attacks on Identity

Low self-esteem can also be caused by experiences that challenge a person's sense of identity or belonging, such as discrimination or exclusion. These experiences can lead to feelings of isolation and disconnection, making it challenging for individuals to develop a positive self-image. According to a study published in the Journal of Personality and Social Psychology, experiences of discrimination can lead to decreased self-esteem.

If you are struggling with low self-esteem, seeking support from a trusted friend, family member, or mental health professional is essential. With the right tools and resources, one can improve self-esteem and develop a positive sense of self-worth.

Have you ever experienced chronic abuse or criticism that has affected your self-esteem?

Have you struggled with social pressures or faced discrimination that has challenged your sense of identity?

By identifying the root causes of low self-esteem, you can address the underlying issues and develop a more positive sense of self-worth.

SIGNS OF LOW SELF-CONFIDENCE AND SELF-ESTEEM

It can be challenging to recognize when someone is struggling with low self-confidence or self-esteem. However, certain signs may indicate that an individual is experiencing these issues. It's important to recognize the signs of low self-confidence and self-esteem, so you can take the necessary steps to improve your mental health and well-being.

Here are some common signs:

1. Negative self-talk

It could be a sign of low self-esteem if you frequently put yourself down, have a negative outlook on yourself or your abilities, and focus on your shortcomings. Negative self-talk can take a toll on your mental health and make it difficult to achieve your goals.

2. Social withdrawal

Those with low self-esteem may avoid social situations or isolate themselves from others. They may feel like they don't belong or aren't worthy of others' attention or affection. Social withdrawal can lead to feelings of loneliness and depression

3. Perfectionism

While having high standards is great, do you find yourself obsessing over every little detail and feel you need to improve? Perfectionism can lead to a fear of failure and cause you to feel like you're never good enough. This can result in a lack of motivation and self-doubt, making it difficult to achieve your goals.

4. Avoidance of challenges

Do you find yourself avoiding new experiences or challenges because you fear failing?

People with low self-confidence may avoid trying new things or taking on new challenges out of fear of failure or feeling inadequate. This can limit your growth and prevent you from reaching your full potential.

5. Seeking external validation

If you constantly seek validation and approval from others, it could be a sign that you lack self-confidence or self-esteem. This can lead to a dependence on others for your sense of self-worth, which can be detrimental to your mental health.

If you or someone you know displays any of these signs, it's crucial to seek help and support. Various interventions can improve low self-confidence and self-esteem, including therapy and self-care practices.

Remember that struggling with low self-confidence or self-esteem is a common issue that many people face, and seeking help does not make you weak or flawed.

Meet Hannah, a 24-year-old who has been struggling with anxiety for years. Hannah's parents divorced when she was young, and as a result, she grew up in a broken home. Her mother, who was dealing with her mental health issues, struggled to provide emotional support to Hannah, leaving her feeling alone and unsupported.

Throughout her teenage years, Hannah's anxiety continued to worsen. She would often find herself consumed with worry over everyday tasks and would struggle to speak up in social situations. Her self-esteem took a hit, and Hannah constantly criticized herself for every mistake she made.

Hannah tried to push herself out of her comfort zone, but her anxiety always held her back. She found herself turning down opportunities that could have benefitted her personal and professional growth, which only made her feel worse about herself. The physical symptoms of her anxiety started to take a toll on her health. Hannah would experience panic attacks that would leave her feeling exhausted and unable to function. Her anxiety affected her relationships with friends and family, and she knew she needed to change.

Hannah decided to seek help and started seeing a therapist. She learned how to manage her anxiety and challenge her negative self-talk through therapy. She also started practicing self-care, such as meditation and exercise, to help alleviate her symptoms.

It wasn't an overnight fix, but Hannah's commitment to improving her mental health paid off. She started feeling more confident in herself and her abilities, and her relationships with others improved as well. Hannah's story is a reminder that no matter what struggles you may be facing, there is always hope for improvement and growth.

Low self-esteem is a common issue that affects many individuals, and it can harm various aspects of life. In our previous discussion, we identified some root causes of low self-esteem, including chronic abuse and criticism, adverse childhood experiences, social pressures, and attacks on identity. It is crucial to address low self-esteem, as it can have detrimental effects on one's mental health, relationships, and personal fulfillment. To improve self-esteem and overcome self-doubt, there are practical strategies that individuals can use. These include identifying and challenging negative self-talk, setting achievable goals, practicing self-care and self-compassion, and seeking support from trusted individuals or professionals.

Before we move on to the next part of your journey, I wanted to share something that helped me measure my self-confidence and what I needed to do to recharge it. Over the years, I became increasingly interested in the idea of journaling. So, I bought myself a notebook, and every day I would mention three things I was grateful for and three things I would want to improve. Now, you would ask– why 3? Well, I wanted to make sure that the number was small so that I would not get lost in the arbitrary nature of the world and how the universe works. I wanted to ensure that the things I was grateful for were truly my accomplishments or valuable milestones.

It's important to remember that building self-esteem is a journey, not an overnight fix. Developing a healthy sense of self takes time and effort but is worth the investment. Anyone can cultivate a positive self-image and live a fulfilling life with dedication and the right tools.

Now, let's turn the page and jump right into the next chapter.

2

BUILDING BLOCKS OF CONFIDENCE

"If you have no confidence in self, you are twice defeated in the race of life. With confidence, you have won even before you have started."

— CICERO

Don't you think Cicero was onto something? Maybe he cracked the code of life? Maybe he looked at the answer that had been lying in front of us all this time. All of it is true. He cracked the code through a key we knew was sitting right before us. Confidence.

Now, every approach and aspect of life has dos and don'ts. Similarly, there are things confident people do and avoid. Some days your mind feels like a prison, and you're a convict, quivering in your jail cell. But what if this cell is your creation? I am sure you must have gone through several articles and self-help posts in order to regain your confidence. But what if I told you the secret lies within the donts instead of the dos. Sounds confusing? Let me break it down for you.

Being a genuine and authentic version of yourself takes courage and confidence. Therefore, confident people do what they want and try to love themselves despite life's flaws and harsh realities. However, confidence is highlighted by all the things you don't do that others expect of you. For example, the popular girl in your group tells you that you cannot dance, so you don't even show up for the annual talent show's tryouts. She is entitled to her own opinion, but her opinion should not dictate your life and decisions. Again, remember Kate Winslet? She never gave up. So, always believe in yourself.

As a teen, you might argue that this is one of the most challenging stages of your life since you're trying to grow, but circumstances, your parents, and many others believe you're too young to mature. In reality, parents of teenagers bear a great deal of responsibility because it is only at this period that they should inculcate self-esteem in their children's thoughts. But, this is more challenging than parents think. For many, adolescence is a time filled with self-doubt, a questionable body image, and insecurity, and it's normal (Morin, 2021). They find it hard to gain confidence due to the experiences that they have had or the constant criticism they go through. But being confident means doing what makes you feel right, even if it's unpopular.

So, what are some things confident people do and don't do?

DO'S & DON'TS FOR SELF-CONFIDENCE

The don'ts of confidence are simple but often too tempting to refrain from. I understand it's hard to turn away from something constantly probing and inciting your curiosity, such as social media, where people often say harsh things to each other. So, even if you want to be a part of it, try to cleanse your feed and exercise discipline. To feel truly confident, you need to believe you are capable. The greatest approach to achieving that belief is to use your abilities and talents – to learn and practice.

Do's Of Self-Confident People

Confidence has the potential to propel you ahead as you discover and develop your strengths. Here are five key things confident people do:

1. They take risks

Self-confident people are not afraid to take risks and try new things. They are willing to step out of their comfort zone and take on challenges.

2. They own their mistakes

Self-confident people don't shy away from admitting their mistakes. They take responsibility for their actions and learn from their errors.

3. They focus on solutions

Self-confident people don't dwell on problems. Instead, they focus on finding solutions and taking action.

4. They embrace failure

Self-confident people understand that failure is a part of the learning process. They don't let failure hold them back and use it as an opportunity to grow.

5. They stand up for themselves

Self-confident people are fearless in asserting themselves and standing up for what they believe in. I wasn't confident enough to stand up to my bully, he fronted it with me, and once I was put in that situation, I had to stand up for myself. I learned from that moment that I needed to be assertive and confident in myself going forward.

Don'ts Of Self Confident People

Here are five things self-confident people don't do:

1. They don't seek validation from others

Self-confident people don't rely on others to validate their self-worth. They know their value and don't need external validation to feel good about themselves.

2. They don't compare themselves to others

Self-confident people don't waste time comparing themselves to others. They focus on their strengths and accomplishments.

3. They don't play it safe

Self-confident people don't play it safe and stay in their comfort zone. They are willing to take risks and step outside their comfort zone to achieve their goals.

4. They don't let others bring them down

Self-confident people don't let negative comments or criticism from others bring them down. They are secure in themselves and their abilities.

5. They don't give up easily

Self-confident people don't give up easily. They are persistent and resilient in the face of challenges and setbacks.

Confidence is pretty elusive, like finding the perfect pair of jeans or getting to inbox zero. But without it, it's all too easy to slide down the rabbit hole of self-doubt and cynicism. And this not only harms our personal lives (anxiety, depression, membership in the lonely hearts club), but it can also have a negative impact on our professional achievement. Therefore you should make it your mission to boost your confidence.

REGAIN YOUR CONFIDENCE

Regaining your confidence can be daunting, but you must make this attempt to regain control of your life.

Here are some ways you can use to boost your confidence:

1. Straighten Up

Mom was right: Sit up straight the next time you notice yourself sagging in your chair or slouching your shoulders! A 2014 study found that sitting with proper posture might boost your self-esteem and mood.

Try it. To appear — and feel — assured and poised, experts recommend expanding your chest and keeping your head level.

2. Jamming

Turning up the music may do wonders for your mind and body. (Tally them! At least 20 health benefits are related to it.). And now, a 2014 study backs up the idea that listening to specific music can make you feel more powerful (Johnson & Duron, 2021).

Also, to quote Meghan Trainor: listening to heavy-bass songs encourages stronger sensations of power than listening to low-bass songs. It's all about the bass (no treble), right?

3. Challenge the Negative Bias

Whenever you engage in self-criticism, pause and search for impartial evidence to support your criticism.

If you cannot remain objective, you may seek the opinion of a trustworthy friend. Try to be the glass half full rather than half empty. It's a common cliche but always try to see the positive side to what you feel is your negative situation. You will likely discover that the majority of your negative self-talk is baseless.

4. Don't Compare Yourself

Avoid comparing yourself to others, and acknowledge that everyone is unique and valuable in their own way (Better Health, 2019). Strive to accept yourself, flaws and all. Rather than dwelling on past grievances and letdowns, focus on the present and live in the moment.

5. Accept Failure

According to executive coach Marshall Goldsmith, Ph.D., author of "What Got You Here Won't Get You There," having a mindset like Michael Jordan, who accepted failure and used it as a learning opportunity, can help develop self-confidence. Plus Jordan famously stated, "I've failed over and over and over again in my life. And that is why I succeed." (Johnson & Duron, 2021) He also had the privilege of playing basketball with Bugs Bunny, which further attests to his expertise.

6. Exercise

Exercise not only offers numerous physical benefits but also has a positive impact on mental health. A study found that physical activity is directly and indirectly connected with self-esteem. Additionally, a 2019 study on health workers revealed that exercise could help improve their self-esteem and prevent uncontrolled eating (Better Health, 2019).

Therefore, exercise is not only helpful in sustaining confidence, but it can also help regain self-assurance when it takes a hit. You can enhance your core confidence by striving to achieve your fitness objectives. Whether you run outside or hit the gym, exercise will leave you feeling good about yourself, irrespective of the physical benefits.

7. Find Hobbies You Like

Finding what you're good at massively adds to your value or worth and will give you confidence! Hobbies can build up your self-esteem and reduce your stress. For example, developing a hobby during hardships can help build yourself back up by giving you a sense of accomplishment every time you progress on that hobby, thus giving you something to feel good about. So, search for things you like to indulge in, such as reading books, cooking or even journaling. Make sure it is something that you enjoy and helps you destress.

8. Be Assertive

Being assertive helps you communicate your needs, wants, feelings, beliefs, and opinions to others directly and honestly while respecting the rights and feelings of others. It is an essential skill for maintaining healthy relationships and achieving personal fulfillment. For example, when you're conversing with your friend, and someone cuts you off in the middle of the conversation, politely redirect the conversation back to yourself. This can also be important when creating and enforcing boundaries.

Slowly and gradually, you will regain your confidence. It's important to remember that this is a time-consuming process. Now, here is the thing about confidence, it's a variable. This means that you will be dealing with many factors when uplifting it. One of the most critical factors contributing to the boost and maximum self-esteem is the environment you expose yourself to. Essentially, you might be dealing with a toxic environment.

What does it look like?

KEEPING GOOD COMPANY

There is no room for mistakes. I'm sure as a teenager, you must have felt the pressure of always excelling. As a young teen, I too jumped on the bandwagon to 'Be Successful, Don't Make Mistakes.' The pressure to be perfect was often heightened during the exam season when I was expected to excel in all my classes, even in subjects that weren't my strongest fronts. I would feel mentally and physically burned out at the end of the year.

Of course, you are going to make mistakes. You are growing and exploring. I was a curious kid, so I would find myself in trouble more often than I care to admit. But curiosity enables you to risk and learn from your mistakes. Unfortunately, most teenagers are confined to square boxes with sharp edges and told never to overstep their comfort zone.

So, why should one even try to get out of their comfort zone?

Stepping outside your comfort zone allows you to have new experiences and participate in activities you haven't done before, all while allowing you to meet new people. If you can do this, you will be open to alternatives you have yet to even consider. In fact, it also helps you find your purpose in life. It might seem risky, but it's a beautiful journey. I recently had this experience when I joined a sports team when I moved to a new city. The first few weeks were awkward as hell, standing by myself waiting for practice to start and feeling like I wasn't fitting in. I was tempted to quit, but I stuck it out for another month and eventually became great friends with everyone on the team, socializing with them at the weekends, and they are now some of my best friends today. Take the chance, and join the class you keep putting off because the grass is greener on the other side of the temporary discomfort.

Does 'don't dwell in toxic environments' ring a bell? If you thought about social media, you were right. Studies have shown that social media has negatively impacted young impressionable minds. Young girls and boys face issues like bullying, which causes them to be depressed and unhappy with their bodies or personalities. It makes teenagers tap into people-pleasing practices, which can have adverse effects in their adulthood, as they might not be able to say 'no' to others, negatively affecting their mental health.

To maintain a healthy lifestyle as an adult, you must learn to set boundaries on relationships and surroundings that do not support your mental and physical health. The people you hung around with from your youth may be going down different more negative paths to you. You might still care deeply for these people, but it's important to focus on yourself and keep at arm's length from anything they're doing that might negatively impact your ambitions.

Did you know a positive correlation exists between your growth as a teenager and the environment you are a part of?

Exactly! It's interesting how studies have shown, time and time again, that childhood trauma and adverse experiences can lead to mental health illnesses for children. But, as you grow up, you gain more control of the environment to thrive in, so take advantage of that.

Hence, changing your environment and the people that surround you regularly can make a big difference in how you perceive yourself. When you walk into your adulthood, work on shifting your environment into a positive light where you are supported, and feel a sense of self-worth. As I moved into my twenties, I was living with friends that were just interested in partying hard at the weekends, relentlessly. I quickly got sucked into this lifestyle when it wasn't me. It took me a few months, but I had to remove myself from that situation because it wasn't having a positive effect on me. I still love the friends I was living with, but this was the boundary I had to set for myself.

According to a 2018 study, people with poor self-esteem tend to surround themselves with negative people. When others criticize them, their words mirror what the person with low self-esteem believes about themselves. And it offers them a twisted feeling of comfort because they believe in, "You see me the same way I see myself" or "They reflect how I feel about myself".

Eventually, that feeling becomes permanent regardless of whether it is true or not. You are sucked into this vicious cycle of self-doubt where you are unable to find your authentic self. Your charm and enigma are lost in the blackhole self-deprivation since you constantly deny yourself the opportunities you deserve.

And why? Because someone said you cannot do it?

But the truth is, you can do it.

Plus, when you let people crowd your space and invade your boundaries, they corrupt your peace. Therefore, mental health experts emphasize creating strict boundaries in relationships and amongst your surroundings. This is majorly prescribed for two reasons. First, having boundaries ensures that your mental health is protected. You are more susceptible to being taken advantage of by your friends or becoming a victim of peer pressure if you have weak boundaries. You might go out of your way to do something for a friend without considering the adverse consequences you might suffer from it. Therefore, boundaries ensure you maintain healthy relationships with people around you. Second, you are able to make informed and sound decisions for yourself without the interruption of someone else.

It is critical to assess the individuals around you. Are you surrounded by people who discreetly criticize you? Examine your physical surroundings as well. Do you live in a chaotic, crowded environment? Perhaps living in a cluttered atmosphere supports your negative beliefs.

So what can you do?

Make it a point to surround yourself with people and things that carry the message that you are sufficient. It will be uncomfortable initially, but it will become easier as your self-esteem grows. Again it all boils down to challenging the negative self-talk that constantly minimizes your achievements and makes you think that your talents are insufficient. That is not true, you need to detach yourself from adverse environments that enable negative self-talk.

Self-compassion can be the key for you; use it to challenge any negative talk that your mind throws your way. Keep an eye on your inner monologue. You will feel horrible about yourself if you continuously tell yourself, "This will never work," or "Everyone will laugh at me."

When you are unduly critical of yourself, or making pessimistic predictions about your chances of success, pause and ask yourself, "Would I say the same things to a friend who was thinking this?" No, you will not. You'd offer some kind words of encouragement. It's much simpler to be good to others than to be kind to oneself. With that in mind, let's move to self-esteem. Like Miss Rihanna once said, when asked what she does when she does not feel confident, she politely replied, 'Fake it till you make it.'

So, act like you are confident. The best part about confidence is that no one knows if it's real, so use it to your advantage. Lastly, if you feel like you cannot bring any change, visit a therapist. It's always better to seek professional help before it's too late.

SOCIAL ANXIETY

Aside from a hostile environment that can have adverse effects on your self-confidence, another factor that I want to mention here is social anxiety. Before we dive into this, it is pretty normal to feel that way. I certainly suffered from this during my teenage years. If you feel like your parents and friends are unable to help, please seek help from a professional.

Now, what is SAD?

Social anxiety disorder (SAD) is also known as social phobia. It is characterized by a constant or intense dread of being evaluated, rejected, embarrassed, or scrutinized by others.

The anxiousness might be extreme and can impact every part of a teen's life. The pandemic has hampered the social development of particular youngsters. Teenagers with social anxiety may have fewer relationships and have difficulty maintaining them. Adolescent social anxiety can also lead to withdrawal (including fear of socializing), isolation, and other mental health problems.

So, how can you deal with it?

It takes more than just affirmations to deal with social anxiety. Your parents and friends will play a massive role in this. However, understand that life is not easy, and you will have to muster all the courage you have to walk through it. It might sound unfair, but when I was younger, I used to think that better days would never find me, but I was wrong. Better days don't find you. You make them happen. You need to understand what you like and what makes you happy, then hold it close to yourself when things get tough. Happiness is a fleeting moment, so catch it, or it'll fly away. I have always been someone who reserved some things for myself, and whenever I wanted to destress, I would often turn to them. For example, I am a huge soccer fan. I passionately follow my favorite football team, Manchester United, because it excites me. During my teenage years, after every exam or trouble in my family, I would switch on the tv or youtube and escape whatever was bothering me. Even though my life has changed for the better, this is a hobby I did not let go of because it's something I do for myself. For you, it might be different, like owning a pet or hanging out with friends, but I am placing emphasis on finding things you feel comfortable with, expanding and exploring your life in every way you can.

Social anxiety holds you back from doing things that can benefit you. I understand because there were moments in my life when I was too nervous to approach people or create a network; therefore, I have created a list of 4 ways you can handle social anxiety yourself:

1. You are not alone

It's easy to think that social anxiety only affects you. But that is far from the truth; I was one of several teens and even young adults who suffered from social anxiety. Days would pass by, and I would not have the energy to walk out of my space. I barely mingled or made any new friends. It crawls inside your soul and makes you feel unimportant, but I am here to tell you that you are not alone in this. You might feel lost, but there is light at the end of every tunnel, and you are not far away. Don't give up on yourself or your abilities to accomplish a lot in life.

2. Go through exposure therapy

Exposure treatment is a method professionals use to help people overcome fear by breaking the pattern of fear and avoidance, a component of cognitive behavioral therapy. It can also be utilized independently. For example, if you have a fear of spiders, you interact with a spider from a distance where you feel comfortable. The idea is that it will expose you to fears and anxieties you're dealing with while in a safe space.

The idea is to sit with the anxiety until it goes away. The same procedure is then repeated until no uneasiness is sensed. Fear or worry is challenged by repeated exposures, and skills to control anxious sensations are created.

3. Fight negative talk

Optimistic and affirmative stances such as 'I will reach my goals by the end of this month' or 'money will find me' or 'I'll pass this test no matter what' are the only way you can fight the negativity that engulfs your mind and soul. Remind yourself that you are talented and charismatic such that people adore you. You are worthy of every chance and opportunity that is guided toward you. By the end of it, you will convince yourself you are enough.

4. Confront uncomfortable situations

When you have social anxiety, entering a new scenario can feel like staring into the deep end of a pool. The temptation is to enter on tiptoe and flee at the first indication of discomfort.

It's sometimes best to dive right in. The water feels nice when the initial shock wears off, and your anxiety about being too cold is no longer relevant. Try not to avoid such situations and step out of your comfort zone.

Moreover, here are some ways parents can also help their teenage children deal with social anxiety:

5. Expose your teen to social situations

If you have a younger teen, make sure they have the opportunity to express themselves in the circumstances, such as ordering at a restaurant or requesting movie tickets. When your teen is confronted with a feared social circumstance, be sure to offer praise and prizes.

Regular exposure to different social events will help your child develop social skills and boost their confidence. This will inevitably include some pushing outside of their comfort zone, but this should be done gradually. A therapist can help with this, and your engagement as a parent is essential.

6. Don't give them special treatment

Treat your teen like any other child and maintain the same standards, but you may need to be more flexible at times. Find activities where they excel, so they may gain confidence, and have them work around the house to make them feel like they are contributing to the family.

7. Listen and offer advice

Listen closely and offer guidance if your adolescent feels comfortable talking to you about their feelings. Tell them that feeling nervous is typical for all teenagers. Remind them of how they have handled difficult situations in the past and express your trust in their capacity to handle them.

8. Make sure they are relaxed

When you have an anxiety disorder, it is crucial to rest and unwind to get away from the tension. Encourage your teen to exercise and engage in relaxing activities such as drawing, painting, playing an instrument, yoga, journaling, or crafts. This will also assist them in better managing their anxiousness. As a parent, you must ensure that your child does not overexert themselves. They should also not become a victim of social pressure, which is essentially something young people deal with nowadays.

Now, you know that your confidence possesses unimaginable power. But what does a healthy relationship with self-esteem look like? Let me put this into perspective for you– Meet Lily; she is a high school student and, like everyone else, often doubts herself. Even though she has always been an outstanding student, when she heard about the Advanced Placement class at her school, she hesitated to sign up. She was consumed by negative self-talk and heavily relied on the experiences of her peers. Her friends who had already taken the class warned her that it was highly challenging and that she might be unable to pass.

Unlike her friends, Lily had a different mindset. She was determined. The sense of I'll try before I admit defeat' helped her conquer her fears. She believed in herself and her abilities and knew she could succeed if she worked hard. So, despite her friends' warnings, she signed up for the class. She refused to get stuck in the trap of peer pressure.

The first few weeks of the class were brutal, just like every new subject a student comes across. The material was complex, and Lily had to work harder than she ever had before to keep up. But she didn't give up. She spent long hours studying, asking questions, and seeking help when needed. This helped her stay on track and meet the deadlines of the course. Eventually, all of her hard work paid off. Lily aced every exam and assignment in the class and ended up earning a top grade. Her friends, who had warned her against taking the class, were amazed and impressed by her accomplishment. Lily learned a valuable lesson from her experience. She realized that sometimes, other people's doubts and fears can hold us back, but we should never let them stop us from pursuing our dreams. If we believe in ourselves and work hard, we can achieve anything we set our minds to.

Ultimately, the critical building blocks of maintaining and rebuilding confidence are positive self-talk and a healthy environment. Being able to convince yourself that you are enough regardless of how many times you have failed enables you to reach for the stars. Dreams with goals always come true, but it is important to surround yourself with supportive people that have your back. But life is unpredictable. It keeps throwing problems at you, so what happens when your leg is stuck in the guilt leg-hold trap? If you are curious about how guilt might affect your self-confidence, keep on reading!

3

THE GUILT POISON

"Nothing is more wretched than the mind of a man conscious of guilt."

— PLAUTUS

A guilty conscience has the ability to manifest itself into a negative version of you. Now, guilt is a tricky thing to deal with. While it serves the purpose of revealing where we went wrong, it can also exist without any reason. So, it loses its meaning when it stays with us for no apparent reason. Therefore, if anything is clear, it's that when guilt isn't a direct outcome of a person's wrongdoings, it can become a real issue, negatively impacting one's well-being.

First of all, nobody is born with thoughts that make you feel guilty. It's not like they just magically appear out of nowhere; these suspicious thoughts stem from abuse, trauma, and anxiety that chains you to self-doubt. If you're feeling guilty without any apparent reason, it's probably linked to something that happened in your past.

Do you know how we all have that little voice that critiques our every move?

Some people have a really loud and mean inner critic. What that voice says and how it says it has a lot to do with the things we were told growing up. Your inner critic tries to overpower the positivity that resurfaces when you are rebuilding your confidence. This happens for several reasons; for example, If you were raised in a family where success was highly valued, chances are your inner critic will be very demanding and put a lot of pressure on you to work harder or face the consequences. This approach trains your inner critic to keep you in check and help you achieve what you are pressured into. However, while your inner critic serves a powerful purpose, it can quickly become a controlling conductor.

Similarly, suppose you grew up in an abusive or neglectful environment. In that case, your inner critic will likely be more harsh and punishing, constantly telling you you're worthless or I'll never succeed. The issue is that these "voices" become ingrained in our personalities over time. They literally transform into us. And, while they may have aided you as children to get out of sticky situations with either your parents or siblings, they now prevent you from attaining your full potential as an adult.

Do you remember SAD? Social anxiety is also a contributing factor to this unwanted sense of guilt. Why does this happen? Anxiety can cloud your judgment of your thoughts and behaviors, making you feel guilty even when you haven't done anything wrong. In fact, as someone who struggles with social anxiety, teenagers are often scared of being judged for doing something outside of the current trend, But the secret lies in being a trendsetter. You would often see old memes and posts resurfacing on social media about a celebrity or someone owning a unique sense of fashion or wearing makeup in a certain way that has now become a trend. Initially, people judged them for being different but eventually loved it as well. The point is that it's important to always do what you love and not pay attention to what people might think about you. People's perceptions are malleable and ever-changing, so don't dwell on something that is temporary. You might think that people are judging you for wearing acid wash jeans, or having braces, etc, but none of that is true! I have learned that we pour so much thought into what people think while they do not care much about us. Other people have so many other things to worry about than what is happening in ours.

You put yourself under unrealistic expectations and pressure from a small percentage of people who will judge you regardless of what you do and who you are, so why not embrace your authentic self? I know that it's easier said than done, but people who care more about their mental health and less about what others think are generally happier.

In fact, you don't have to do something wrong to experience guilt when you are exposed to a hostile environment. As we discussed in the previous chapter, a malicious environment can adversely affect your confidence. It does so by inducing unwanted guilt in your mindset. It's possible to feel guilty just because of social pressure. Some people are very critical and judgmental, and if you feel the need to always live up to their expectations, guilt can become a real issue for you. This kind of guilt is often linked to your sense of self-worth, self-esteem, and ability to establish healthy boundaries.

TYPES OF GUILT

With that being said, did you know that there are different kinds of guilts? I was surprised by the information, and it helped me understand my tendencies better. Here are four major types of guilt that everyone should know about:

1. Natural

Feeling guilty after doing something wrong is a natural and common reaction. This type of guilt can be helpful because it can prompt you to take steps to fix what you've done and make positive changes in the future. For instance, you might apologize for your actions or change any problematic behaviors. However, if you don't address these actions in a way that allows you to move on, you may end up with prolonged feelings of guilt that can disrupt your life.

2. Maladaptive guilt

There are instances when individuals experience guilt for things that are out of their control. They may feel guilty for not taking action to prevent something that they couldn't have predicted. Despite the fact that there was nothing they could have done, they still experience intense feelings of shame, regret, and guilt.

3. Guilty Thoughts

It's common for individuals to occasionally have negative or inappropriate thoughts, but some may start feeling guilty about having such thoughts. Even if they don't act on them, they may worry that they will in the future or that others will discover their "wrong" thoughts.

4. Existential guilt

This kind of guilt can be complex and typically stems from things like feeling guilty about injustices or not living up to one's values. One form of existential guilt is survivor's guilt, where someone may feel guilty for doing well when others they care about are not. This can occur after surviving a disaster or accident in which others were harmed, but it can also happen when others experience misfortune while you do not.

Now you know that a guilt complex is a persistent belief that you have done or will do something wrong. You also know that It's the result of past experiences and relationships and can significantly negatively impact a person's mental health and well-being. So, how does it play out?

Plagued With Guilt

When someone is dealing with complex guilt, they tend to replay past situations in their head, searching for any mistakes they may have made. This can cause a lot of anxiety and depression, leading to feelings of hopelessness, isolation, and emotional paralysis. Negative self-talk and a loss of confidence can lead to even more guilt, creating a tough cycle to break. Feeling like everything is your fault can also impact your self-esteem and feelings about yourself, which can be connected to mental health problems and a lower quality of life.

Additionally, it can lead to perfectionism, making handling mistakes and failures challenging. Guilt complexes can also harm your relationships with others. When you feel intense guilt and blame yourself for everything, you can become overly critical or doubt yourself to the point of being unable to function. This can cause you to distance yourself from people you care about because you fear making mistakes or failing. It can also be challenging for your loved ones to understand what you're going through and offer support because they might have already reassured you that you're not to blame. It puts a strain on your relationships as well. You also experience fatigue or burnout easily; these are not co-factors of guilt but rather of anxiety or depression that walk in line with guilt. Therefore, it's important to note that guilt does not only impact a person's mental health. Ultimately, the burden of guilt can have substantial consequences for both mental and physical health. This might make you think, is guilt good for me? If not, why does it even exist?

IS GUILT GOOD?

The guilt system was functionally designed to keep us from injuring those we care about and motivate us to do better in the future. Guilt can make us more compassionate and generous. Placing costs on individuals who care about your well-being is indirectly costly for the individual as it drives them away from us. Putting conditions within relationships eventually drains the love from them. The guilt system is intended to identify the imposition of this harm, halt it, and remedy it.

Similarly, shame informs us when we act in ways that may cause others to devalue us and refuse to help us. As a result, natural selection favors those who experience remorse and shame. Now, revisiting the first part of your curious question; is it good for us?

In some cases, guilt can be helpful or "adaptive," according to researchers. Feeling guilty can indicate that our moral compass is working and that we can differentiate between right and wrong, which helps us interact and care for one another. When bad things happen to others, guilt can motivate us to engage in repetitive behaviors, such as extending kindness or offering resources. Guilt can also inspire us to apologize for our mistakes and minimize societal inequalities. In romantic relationships, guilt can encourage us to treat our partners well and make up for any missteps.

Additionally, when we see global crises in the news, guilt can prompt us to donate money or volunteer, especially when we witness the generosity of others. Overall, guilt can inspire positive action and pay it forward. However, if taken too far can also lead to adverse effects.

Guilt can also have harmful effects and become "maladaptive," Do you remember? It's one of the types of guilt that we discussed earlier. Two types of guilt that can be especially detrimental are free-floating and contextual guilt. Free-floating guilt is a general feeling of guilt where you believe you are a terrible person. On the other hand, contextual guilt is when you take too much responsibility for something, such as continuously trying to help an ex in all aspects of their life because you feel guilty for ending the relationship.

Now, moving to the causal link between overthinking and guilt- what are the connecting dots between them?

GUILT AND OVERTHINKING

Overthinking and guilt are often linked in a symbiotic relationship. Now, what is that? A symbiotic relationship is established when two elements favor each other; in our example, it's a hypothetical relation but important to note. When we feel guilty, we may obsess about the incident or action that produced it, replaying and analyzing it in our brains. This might result in overthinking and a downward spiral of opposing ideas and emotions. Overthinking can exacerbate guilt by causing us to blame ourselves excessively or to envisage worst-case situations. This, in turn, can cause feelings of anxiety and despair, making it more difficult to break out from the pattern. Overthinking might also keep us from taking proper action to solve the matter, perpetuating our feelings of guilt. This lethal combination can make it difficult to let go of previous mistakes or regrets, trapping us in a loop of guilt and rumination. In our minds, we may replay events, seeking ways we could have done things better or wishing we had acted differently. This persistent focus on the past might make moving on and letting go of the guilt we feel difficult.

GUILT-FREE

You must be thinking, is there any way I can get out of this vicious trap of guilt? Honestly, there are countless ways you can untie the knot with guilt, but here are my five favorite, tried and tested ways to overcome the feeling of guilt:

1. Positive Affirmations

Let me start with something that has occasionally found focus within our previous chapter, positive self-talk. Positive talk can be practiced in several ways, so my personal favorite is positive affirmations. Start your day by reciting positive affirmations to yourself shortly after you wake up while still in bed. Maintain the current tense and utilize the first person in your affirmations. For example, I am well and affluent and welcome all great things into my life.

2. Forgive Yourself

To be free of guilt, you must forgive yourself and others. It is critical to understand that forgiving is not the same as accepting pain. Instead, it's about taking care of yourself so you can move on with your life without being held back by guilt or the person who injured you. You have made and will continue to make mistakes as a human being. Forgiveness is the key to allowing yourself to live a more positive life.

3. Learn from the past

Mistakes can sometimes come at a high cost, jeopardizing cherished relationships and close friendships. The burden of guilt, coupled with the sorrow of losing someone or something dear, often feels inescapable. However, in order for you to move forward, acceptance is essential. Merely dwelling on the past and replaying memories won't mend what has happened. Though you cannot change the events by imagining different outcomes, you can always extract valuable lessons

Firstly, it's crucial to examine what led to the mistake. Take time to explore the triggers that influenced your actions and the emotions that pushed you over the edge.

Next, consider what you would do differently if faced with a similar situation now. Reflect on how you've grown and what new insights you've gained from your experiences.

Lastly, analyze your actions and discern what they reveal about your character. Identify specific behaviors that may require improvement and be open to working on them.

Remember, self-reflection and learning from the past are powerful tools for personal growth and building stronger relationships in the future.

4. Quality v Quantity

In order to avoid feeling guilty about not doing enough of certain things, try to shift your focus to appreciate the time you spend on them. For example, if you feel guilty about not spending enough time with your family, make a conscious effort to be fully present and engaged during your next activity together. This may involve turning off your phone or other distractions and really focusing on the experience. By taking these steps, you can help alleviate some of the guilt and feel more satisfied with the time you spend on these important activities.

5. Talk to people you trust

Typically, people have difficulty discussing guilt. After all, it's not easy to bring up a regrettable error. This means guilt can separate you, and loneliness and isolation can make healing difficult. You may be concerned that people will judge you for what happened, but this is not always true. In truth, you might find that your loved ones offer significant support. Those who genuinely care about you will often show kindness and compassion when you share your unpleasant or challenging feelings. Expressing your guilt can also alleviate tension and bring a sense of relief. Moreover, when friends and family open up about their own experiences, it helps you feel less isolated in your struggles. Remember, nearly everyone has experienced regrets, making them more empathetic and understanding of your feelings of guilt

6. See a Therapist

Sometimes, it's hard to shake off feelings of guilt, especially when it's linked to intrusive thoughts, depression, or traumatic experiences. Feeling apprehensive about discussing your guilt with others is normal if you fear being judged. I want you to understand that having low self-confidence, social anxiety, and depression is common. I experienced them as well. As a teenager, speaking to your close friends and family about everything cluttering your head might seem daunting. It's best that you refer to a professional that will endorse confidentiality and take a solution-oriented approach with you. However, ignoring these emotions can make things worse in the long run. You need to confront and process them.

If you feel miserable, ponder your mistakes, and struggle to be present with yourself and others, it might be time to consider professional help. Working with a therapist or mental health professional can be beneficial. They can help you identify the root causes of your guilt, teach you effective coping skills, and encourage you to practice self-compassion. This reminds me of Lily.

She was my classmate in 8th grade. Lily struggled with self-confidence during her teenage years. However, this lack of confidence was also fueled by guilt. Despite being an excellent student and having supportive friends and family, she often felt like she wasn't good enough. She compared herself to others; no matter how hard she tried, she always felt like she fell short. It was as if she was stuck in a cycle of guilt and self-inflicted doubt that hindered her growth.

During the mid-8th grade, Lily and her friends went to a party, and they all tried out new things and tested each other's limits. Lily and her friends started playing spin the bottle. When the bottle stopped at her, she was dared to do something that would break the girl code, so she made a mistake - she kissed her friend's boyfriend. Lily immediately regretted what she had done and felt even worse about herself.

As the days passed, Lily's self-doubt grew stronger, and the guilt of her mistake made it even harder for her to feel confident. She felt like she was a terrible person and that everyone judged her for her actions. She withdrew from her friends, stopped participating in extracurricular activities, and even struggled to focus on her studies.

One day, Lily's mom noticed how much her daughter had changed and encouraged her to discuss what was happening. Lily finally opened up and shared her self-confidence struggles and how her mistake had made things worse. Her mom listened without judgment and reminded her that everyone makes mistakes, which doesn't define who she is.

With her mom's support, Lily began to work on her self-confidence. She started writing down her positive attributes and accomplishments, which helped her see herself more positively. She also started practicing positive self-talk and made an effort to stop comparing herself to others.

Over time, Lily's self-confidence began to grow, and she was able to repair her friendships and regain her focus on her studies. She learned that self-confidence takes practice and it's okay to make mistakes as long as she learns from them and continues to grow. Eventually, by the end of 9th grade, Lily was excited about the opportunities ahead of her.

THINK ABOUT IT

I like to consider guilt as quicksand. Once you are in it, you keep sinking in. Have you ever felt stuck in an obnoxious cycle of self-doubt and low confidence? If that is the case, I have enlisted some of my favorite, tried and tested ways to help you reclaim your sense of confidence. Remember, you own the power to change your life! All in all, to boost your self-confidence, you need to shun the chains of guilt. However, an interesting element of self-confidence revolves around…

4

THE SCIENCE OF EMOTIONS

"I don't want to be at the mercy of my emotions. I want to use them, to enjoy them, and to dominate them."

— OSCAR WILDE

Our mind is a paradox, and our body is a prisoner to its intuition. Sometimes we misinterpret the signals sent to us from our mind. Our body cannot process and decipher the code often delivered to it. But, if only we could understand how our mind works and discover the truth underneath thousands of neural pathways. I wonder if we are merely a puppet and our minds a puppeteer. Scientists have tried to unearth the mind-boggling mystery of emotions and their uncontrollability. While people argue that emotions play a massive role in making people make unreasonable decisions; however, emotions also ensure that humans are subjected to empathy and compassion. Naturally, emotions make us human.

Let's address the elephant in the room, are emotions good or not?

We must redress the question into 'Are emotions conscious of unconscious processes?' Emotions are an unconscious process that alerts our body about a problem but remains dormant when everything is alright. While unrelated, conscious emotions are often associated with feelings (something we will explore later in this chapter). You might experience conscious emotions when you are aware of a situation you encounter through the plethora of your experiences. For example, fear; if you are not mindful that you are afraid, you hardly ever recognize it, but if you do, you are feeling fear. Your emotions are overwhelming because you have yet to fully understand their power and how to use them to your advantage.

Have you heard the phrase, 'If you feel like you shouldn't take a risk, that is exactly when you should take it' While this is an awfully confusing statement often used by educators and mentors, it implies that your emotions are usually triggered when you are facing a challenging situation. They are strategically placed in your body by your mind to help you survive or protect yourself from difficult situations. For example, you want to explore new friend groups in your school, but you stop yourself from talking to anyone new because of this overwhelming feeling that storms in your chest. You feel like you are out of breath and sweating profusely– that is anxiety triggered by your emotional distress. You see, our mind has evolved over the course of several years to help us survive. But, often, we need to explore difficult situations to grow, which is why people must control their emotions. How can you master your emotions? Before we get to the juicy bits, I know you are intrigued. I want us to explore what emotions are in their simplest form.

BASICS OF EMOTIONS

Emotions are a natural and valuable way our bodies respond to things, and they play a significant role in how we live our lives. They are expressed in the theater of our bodies through facial expressions, body language, posture, and things happening inside us, like heart rate or blood pressure changes. Plus, all of these physical reactions get sent back to the brain through different neural channels as well as humoral channels by bypassing the receptive signaling. Don't be afraid of the big words I just used. Simply put, emotions depend on experiential, behavioral, and psychological elements that can also act as a stimulus. Have you heard people talk about the 'emotional response to situations'? Well, emotions are how we as humans deal with circumstances that are personal to us.

Ironically, your emotions are your strength but also your weakness. Isn't it interesting how something we cannot see but only feel affects our actions? But, there is a catch often, emotions are confused with feelings. They are not interchangeable. In fact, they are poles apart.

You need to distinguish emotions from feelings to understand the inner workings of your body. So, how can you identify emotion? Let me simplify it for you–

When you experience any primary emotions, such as sadness, happiness, anger, fear, surprise, or disgust, they express your experiences. This can be observed by another person; that is, emotion at its finest.

What does this mean?

Let me give you an example, If I went into a haunted house, what would I feel? Fear right? So, my body quivers, and I feel panic tightening my chest. Our bodies often state our emotions in the shape of reactions.

On the contrary, feelings are responsive perceptions of the changes triggered within your body due to the emotional response. So, feelings are a consequence of emotions, in a way. Besides, feelings usually deal with subtle changes in how your cognitive apparatus functions (Cherry, 2022).

Most of what happens when we feel an emotion happens without us even realizing it. Sometimes, our body might already be showing signs of anger before we know what's causing it. This physical reaction is automatic and mostly determined by our genetic makeup, responding not to a specific trigger but to certain types of things.

For example, in a more technical sense, when you are afraid, angry, or even happy, you produce withdrawal or approach behaviors depending on the emotion at play (Juby, 2018). This reaction has been preserved through evolution because it proved to be advantageous when it came to survival. We have inherited this system for sorting out what is good and bad for our mind and body in order to preserve ourselves.

TYPES OF EMOTIONS

The power of such nonconscious processing is enormous. So, now you know what emotion is. Let's move on to the types of emotions. At the outset of this whole discussion, there are two main categories; negative and positive emotions. These categories further advance into complex emotional reactions and outbursts depending on the intensity of the triggering cause. I am sure you already know all the emotions I will list, so why am I even revisiting them? Only to create a context for the leading pool of knowledge that we will dive into later.

So, how many emotions are there?

Paul Ekman, a psychologist and esteemed researcher, conducted an in-depth study of emotions. He engaged with more than 100 experts, gathering their insights to develop the Atlas of Emotions. This innovative online interactive tool categorizes emotions into five primary groups:

- Anger
- Fear
- Sadness
- Disgust
- Enjoyment

It's crucial to keep in mind that this is merely one way of categorizing emotions. For instance, a study from 2017 proposes the existence of 27 emotion categories. However, Ekman's idea of five primary types of emotions provides a valuable framework for simplifying the complexity of all feelings. Before we look at the five main categories and master how to practice and regulate them let's understand how emotions occur.

All emotions start with a subjective experience, also known as a stimulus, but what exactly does it mean? While all people display basic emotions, regardless of culture or background, the experience that causes them can be profoundly subjective.

Subjective experiences can be as basic as seeing a color or as profound as losing a loved one or getting married. No matter how strong the experience is, it can elicit a wide range of feelings in a single person, and each person's emotions may differ. For example, one individual may feel rage and regret over the death of a loved one, while another may feel intense sadness. However, what triggers our emotions varies from one person to another, shaped by a combination of shared evolution, cultural influences, and individual life experiences. Hence, while we cannot select the feelings we experience, we can choose how we respond to them through emotional awareness. Here's a look at what each of these five categories involves and how to deal with them:

1. Sadness

This emotion usually arises for several reasons, mostly due to rejection or loss. Be empathetic when you find yourself mourning or seeing someone close to you is sad. Whether you're in the process of healing from a loss or a breakup or failure to achieve a goal, accepting your loss can help you accept and work through it. Everyone grieves differently, so do what seems best for you. It may help to talk about your pain, but it may also help to sit with your feelings or express them creatively. In fact, do something good. While Phoebe from friends might argue that 'doing something good' is not entirely an act of selflessness, and we might agree. But since it makes you feel good, it's all right!

2. Fear

Fear happens when you sense any threat. Depending on that perceived threat, fear can range from mild to severe. If you're scared of something, whether it's a serious debate, meeting new people, or driving, it's normal to want to avoid it. Nonetheless, this can frequently aggravate your fear. Instead, try to confront your fear in a safe manner. For example, if you develop a phobia of driving, immediately get back in your car and drive again. If it helps, stay close to home at first, but don't ignore it. When the effect of fear becomes overwhelming, try to distract yourself by doing something interactive. But you need to treat fear logically. Think about how it can harm you and how you can avoid it.

3. Anger

Anger usually occurs when you are unjustly treated. It happens more often than we would care to admit, right? But regulating and managing anger properly is essential to avoid an outburst. You need to exercise patience and self-control to not channel your anger on someone who does not deserve it. Your anger should be your motivation, strength, and power. Many people's aggressive reaction leads to unredeemable consequences; therefore, be careful about how you express your anger.

4. Disgust

Disgust is commonly experienced as a reaction to unpleasant or unwanted situations. Similar to anger, this emotion serves as a protective mechanism, helping you avoid things that could be harmful or undesirable. Feeling uncomfortable when confronted with something you fear or don't understand is natural. Many people, for example, dislike being near sick people. When someone you care about does something that offends or disgusts you, you may withdraw, push them away, or become upset. Try chatting with that person instead. If your sister smokes, for example, avoid coughing loudly or making pointed remarks about the smell of tobacco. Instead, tell her that cigarette smoke makes you sick and that you are worried about her health. Offer to assist her in quitting or work with her to get support.

5. Enjoyment

It's this feeling of excitement that usually occurs when you are happy. Try to regulate it by keeping a positive mindset and exercising compassion. Have happy thoughts in moments of despair. I know that life can be stressful and challenging, but take a moment to enjoy it and cherish each memory. Life is full of beautiful moments, such as long car rides with friends, going to a festival, or watching a movie. It's all about stopping and thoroughly enjoying these moments.

Our emotions play a massive role in how we feel about things. Have you ever felt sad about something rude your friend said to you? As you have previously explored in this chapter, our emotions are subtle triggers to situations that either make us uncomfortable or happy. Emotions help you communicate how you are feeling when you cannot find the right words to articulate them.

EMOTIONS AND THOUGHTS

Since we are thinking about happy thoughts, is there a link between emotions and thoughts?

Interesting question!

Yes, thoughts and emotions are linked. They are two sides of the same coin and influence each other. Thoughts can trigger emotions, and emotions can shape our thoughts. For example, having negative thoughts about yourself can lead to feelings of sadness or anxiety. On the other hand, if you feel happy or excited about something, it can lead to positive thoughts and perceptions. Our thoughts and emotions work together to help us interpret and respond to the world around us. We tend to believe that emotions are just "part of us" and can't be changed. Research, however, has established that emotions are malleable. For example, this might be due to a change in your external circumstances (e.g., dysfunctional family) or a change in your focus (e.g., initially, you wanted to excel in your classes but got stuck in high school drama). This also includes reassessing a situation (the upcoming test is a learning opportunity, not an assessment of my personal worth). How we choose to spend our life dramatically influences how we feel every day.

In fact, a study conducted by Sonja Lyubomirsky and other positivity researchers discovered that your "set point," or heredity, determines 50% of your happiness, and your environment decides 10% (finances, health, and living situation). The other 40% is based upon your intentional efforts to become happier, meaning you have a big say in how you feel.

Certain types of mental training, such as mindfulness or positive thinking, can affect our perceptions of the world and make us feel calmer, more resilient, and happier. Other researchers have identified many other helpful attitudes—such as forgiveness, gratitude, and kindness—that can be cultivated with practice. If you are aware of your thoughts and emotions, you can choose to change them!

NEGATIVE EMOTIONS

Emotions such as anger, frustration, and fear, usually referred to as "negative emotions," are typical aspects of being human. Although they can generate stress and are generally considered negative feelings, they can also be good to experience. Instead of dismissing them, it is preferable to deal with them constructively. There are several reasons why regulating these emotions without denying them is preferable.

Dealing with negative emotions is not as simple as avoiding them because it can worsen things. And on the flip side, you can't just let these feelings take over your life and mess everything up. For instance, if you let anger control you, it can ruin relationships. Did you know that negative emotions adversely impact your physical health?

Having negative attitudes and feeling helpless or hopeless can lead to long-term stress. This can upset the balance of hormones in our bodies, reduce the chemicals that make us happy, and harm our immune system. All of this can shorten our lifespan. Scientists have found that stress can even speed up aging by shortening our telomeres, which are the "end caps" of our DNA strands.

When we don't manage our anger well or keep it bottled up inside (known as hostility), it can cause a bunch of health problems as well. These include high blood pressure, heart disease, digestive issues, and infections. Your mental health is tied to your physical health; I urge you to be kind to yourself and shed the negative emotions. As discussed earlier in this chapter, negative emotions can cause stress. We have established that, right? No one enjoys feeling uncomfortable, so it is reasonable to want to avoid uncomfortable emotions, yet the dangers of mismanaged stress are real. However, some people believe that these emotions will stay forever or that the sentiments themselves are the problem. That's not true; negative emotions erupt due to several external triggers you explored in previous chapters, such as memories, people, trauma, etc. This feeling of sadness and hollowness will pass.

Interestingly, negative feelings can be seen in a positive light as they are beneficial because they can also send us messages. For example:

- Anger and anxiety are indicators that something in our lives requires change, and they may signal a potential threat to our well-being.
- Fear serves as a call to enhance our safety and security measures.
- Frustration or resentment act as motivators, prompting us to address necessary changes within our relationships.

Negative emotions alert us that something needs to change and motivate us to make that change. But how can you identify negative emotions?

IDENTIFY NEGATIVE EMOTIONS

Your emotional bandwidth is entirely different from your siblings or friends, majorly because humans, while being similar, have their unique sense of self. Talking about your emotions in therapy is best, but some teenagers cannot afford or rely on therapy. So what can you use if therapy isn't something you want to go through? You can try out soul searching.

I believe that introspection can be helpful for everyone, even those who won't seek therapy. In this case, how can we identify and comprehend our emotions? And how can we determine our emotions' influence on our actions?

1. Take your emotional temperature

Have you ever tried asking yourself a few questions to understand your emotions better? It might help you gain some clarity. Here are a few questions that could guide you:

Firstly, what emotions do you notice within yourself? There could be several, so take your time to think about it. Then, which one stands out the most to you? Please don't shy away from describing it in detail. Even if you initially answer with something vague like "fine," try to go deeper and ask yourself what "fine" means to you.

When did you start feeling this way? I suggest writing down your questions and answers in a notebook so that you can refer back to them later. Take your time with this process and describe each emotion thoroughly, even the pleasurable ones. It's also essential to recognize what brings joy to your life, as it can help create a sense of balance during tough times.

As you explore these questions, you might uncover other thoughts and memories you haven't thought of before. So, be open to surprises along the way.

2. Identify stressors

Firstly, ask yourself what could be causing this feeling. Then, try to analyze your daily life, breaking it down into days, weeks, and months. Look out for events, thoughts, or even dreams you may have ignored because you cannot control them. This is a common mistake because the lack of control itself can trigger an emotional reaction.

If you're having trouble pinpointing the feeling, try examining your behavior and daily routine instead. Here are a few questions that could help you:

How is your home life? Are you getting along with your partner, children, parents, and siblings?

How do you feel about your school or university's academic pressure? Are you enjoying it, and do you get along with your friends and family? What do they say about you, and do you agree with it?

Also, look for patterns in your life that may be forming. Take the time to explore them, and ask yourself what they tell you.

3. Notice if you start judging what you feel

You might find yourself saying, "I have no reason to feel bad, anxious, or depressed." But it's important to wait for an outcome before jumping to conclusions. We often blame ourselves for our feelings, but in reality, life events generate feelings - they just happen. Although we can choose which feelings to focus on, we don't have control over feeling or not feeling them. Our job is to identify and allow them to exist (Pflug, 2022).

I relied on headspace meditation to distract myself. Think of all the thoughts that cross your mind as busy traffic. The key is to sit still and observe the traffic instead of running after a specific thought or nitpicking them.

Sounds simple enough?

But it's a busy road, and it's easy for you to get lost in trying to track and unload a negative thought.

So, what do you do?

Always come back to observing. This way, you will understand which thought affects you the most and why. Hence your mind does not wander and fall into negative thoughts; instead, it achieves peace.

While some people may be able to push away negative thoughts, others may find it impossible. Dismissing anxious or depressed feelings is usually ineffective and can even be harmful. It can lead to the belief that one is weak or a failure for not being able to control their fear.

Therefore, it's essential to be understanding and patient with oneself. Feeling scared or anxious in the face of uncertainty or threat is okay. Instead of denying these feelings, it's important to acknowledge them and give them space. Everything is now falling into place for you when it comes to emotions and confidence. They are intertwined.

SELF-CONFIDENCE AND EMOTIONS

Boosting our self-confidence involves getting to know ourselves better and accepting who we are. A crucial part of this is recognizing, accepting, and experiencing our emotions.

We need to approach our emotions with openness, curiosity, and without judgment, allowing ourselves to feel them fully. Sometimes we may feel guilty about our emotions and think we're supposed to always be happy, but this is not true. Moreover, you must understand how you can control your emotions.

Don't be afraid of our emotions because we can trust ourselves more by understanding and naming them. We become more confident in our identity and know we are good enough.

HOW TO CONTROL YOUR EMOTIONS

Your emotions are a freeway to what you're experiencing and how you are processing your moments in life. It can be hard to master control over your emotions, majorly because they are unpredictable. As you saw at the beginning of this chapter, our mind is a complex organ. So, how can you really control your emotions? Here are my five tried and tested ways to manage your emotions:

1. Aim for Regulation, Not Repression

You can't dial in your emotions (if only it were that simple!). But consider for a second that you could manage your emotions this way.

You wouldn't want to leave them on full power all the time. You also don't want to turn them completely off.

When you suppress or repress emotions, you prevent yourself from experiencing and expressing feelings. This might occur purposefully (suppression) or inadvertently (repression).

When learning to control your emotions, make sure you're not simply pushing them under the rug. Finding a happy medium between overpowering feelings and no emotions at all is essential for healthy emotional expression.

2. Accept Your Emotions

To improve your emotional management, try downplaying your feelings to yourself.

When you hyperventilate after excellent news or collapse on the floor sobbing and shouting because you can't locate your keys, it may seem useful to tell yourself, "It's not that big of a deal; I'll be okay" This ensures that while your feelings are valid, you do not let them cloud your judgment.

Accepting emotions as they arise allows you to become more at ease with them. Increasing your comfort level with overwhelming emotions allows you to experience them completely without reacting in severe, counter-productive ways.

3. Know When To Express

Intense emotions are appropriate in some situations but not in others. It's normal to cry uncontrollably when you lose a loved one or to scream and punch your pillow when dealing with a breakup. However, there are times when it's important to exercise restraint. For example, yelling at your boss in response to an unfair disciplinary action won't resolve the issue.

To navigate these situations, being aware of your surroundings and the context is essential. Recognizing when it's appropriate to express your emotions and when to hold back can help you handle your feelings effectively.

4. Stay on top of stress

When you're experiencing a lot of stress, it can be challenging to manage your emotions effectively. Even individuals who are typically adept at controlling their emotions may find it more difficult during times of high tension and stress.

To make your emotions more manageable, it can be helpful to reduce stress or find more beneficial ways to cope with it. Mindfulness practices such as meditation can assist with stress management. Meet up with people you enjoy being around; they ground you in stressful situations as they aren't experiencing what you're going through themselves.

5. Give yourself a break

According to Botnick, taking a step back from overwhelming emotions can help you respond to them in a logical manner. This could imply physically withdrawing oneself from a distressing circumstance or psychologically creating some distance by distracting yourself. For example, let's say you are arguing with your friend about something. Since you both cannot find common ground, the conversation becomes intense. So, you withdraw, ask for space to recollect your thoughts, and then try to reason.

It's vital not to entirely block or avoid your emotions, but it might be beneficial to briefly distract yourself until you feel more prepared to deal with them. Just remember to return and address them afterward. Healthy distractions should only be used for a short period of time.

Going for a stroll, viewing a hilarious video, talking to a loved one, or spending time with your pet are all examples of healthy distractions.

All in all, when you can regulate your emotions, you find strength within yourself to overcome all the negative talk that pulls you down. Emotions, when appropriately managed, help in boosting self-confidence. Our mind is a complicated entity, but once you are able to understand the intricacies of how your psychological pathway deals with your emotions, you will be able to resolve 20% of your confidence issues. But it is also vital for you to understand external factors that contribute to the deterioration of your mental health. You must have guessed the factors by now; I am hinting toward one in particular. So, if you are curious to find out, keep on reading!

TEENAGE AFFECTION FOR SOCIAL MEDIA

"Don't use social media to impress people; use it to impact people."

— DAVE WILLIS

These wise words from Dave Willis have more depth than one can imagine. Social media has been subjected to criticism since its evolution in 2016. With the fall of Facebook and the rise of other platforms such as Instagram and Tiktok, there is a lot to unpack. Ironically, people are stuck in limbo regarding social media; its addictive nature stretches people into its vortex of fake pictures and filtered posts. Its vast access to the audience also enables people to create awareness. It's plausible to believe that you have the power to shift your narrative, especially regarding how you use social media.

As a teenager, you are yet to see the treacheries of the world. I know it might sound condescending, but it is a difficult truth. The world is not as simple as black and white; people constantly try to find ways to manipulate young children. I recently came across a horrifying truth– Youtube Kids have some adult-themed content that minors (5-10 year-olds) are exposed to. All while the parents are under the impression that their child is watching Peppa Pig, they are unaware that there are several defective versions of the innocent show. This was highly concerning for me because children are conditioned to think negatively from a young age. As you grow up, it's important for you to properly navigate through the traps of social media. It's also important to understand that social media can adversely affect your mental health and therefore lower your self-confidence. The more time you spend on social media surfing through adverts and carefully constructed content, your chances of regaining control of your confidence are lowered. This leads me to an important question– How long do you use social media?

Did you check your screen time?

THE WEB OF SOCIAL MEDIA

Social media has a web of lies that's easy to get tangled in, that is not to say that it's all bad, but if you are not careful, you can get caught up in the drama and photoshopped images. The more time you spend on any social media platform, the more your time is consumed being unproductive. As a teenager, social media was the heart of my life; all my friends were on it, and I did not want to be left out. However, when I spent hours scrolling through random people's feeds, my productivity levels dropped because I felt terrible after switching off my phone. Why did I feel bad? Well, majorly because I was exposed to these fake lives that people lived and all the fun they had all while I was at home doing my homework. But as I stepped into my 20s, I realized it was all a facade, and I didn't actually miss out on anything. I now take downtime from social media for months at a time, deleting my personal social media apps such as Instagram, Facebook, and Twitter. It takes a few days to break the pattern of searching where they are amongst all the other apps, but after a day or two, you break the habit and realize very quickly how little you miss them.

Do you know how much time an average teen spends on social media?

In a survey conducted by Real Research Media, almost 55% of teenagers in the United States believe they spend an appropriate amount of time on social media. In comparison, 36% feel they spend too much time on these platforms. Only a small percentage of teens (8%) believe they spend too little time on social media. When asked about the difficulty of giving up social media, 54% of teens say it would be challenging, while 46% believe it would be relatively easy. Do you see how addictive social media is? I'm sure you must also find it difficult to completely eliminate social media from your life, but what if I told you, you didn't have to? We'll get into it later!

Girls are more likely than boys to express difficulty in giving up social media. Older teens also report more difficulty giving up social media, with 58% of 15 to 17-year-olds finding it challenging compared to 48% of 13 to 14-year-olds. On the other hand, a quarter of teen boys believe that giving up social media would be effortless, while only 15% of teen girls feel the same way.

In a more normative sense,

- 38.16% of teenagers believe they spend more than 8 hours daily on these platforms.

- Another 13.39% of teenagers spend 7 to 8 hours on social media daily,
- 11.59% believe they spend 5 to 6 hours.
- 10.7% feel that social media time is limited to 3 to 4 hours.
- 8.34% feel they spend 1-2 hours or less than an hour.

This distribution shows that the average time lies between 8-10 hours. Spending such a significant amount of time somewhere must take a toll on your mental health, right? It does!

IMPACT OF SOCIAL MEDIA

Social media can be a lifesaver for teens who feel isolated or marginalized. Since it helps teens feel more connected. But, social media can have detrimental effects on your mental health. Is the combination of teenagers and social media platforms beneficial, or does it harm their well-being? Why is social media considered harmful? This has become a contentious issue in discussing the impact of social media on teenagers, as studies have produced diverse findings.

Teenagers are being heavily influenced by the internet, leading to a rise in their use of social media. This increased access to social media is negatively impacting young people's mental, physical, and social development. Nowadays, teenagers are more interested in using social media on their phones than in participating in physical activities or socializing with peers. Overall, the digital world has a significant and early impact on teens. While social media has allowed for global interaction, the vast amount of content on these platforms is not effectively regulated, which can have both positive and negative consequences. Social media is often criticized for making people compare their lives with others.

Several researchers propose that the rise in social media and screen usage during adolescence could be responsible for these changes. The surveyed adolescents who spent more time on social media tended to report more mental health issues. In comparison, those who spent more time engaging in real-life activities, such as in-person social interaction, sports, exercise, homework, and print media, were less likely to report these issues.

Over the past decade, numerous studies have supported this theory by linking teenagers' social media use to increased depression. These studies demonstrate that the frequency of social media use by teenagers is directly related to their mental health. For instance, in a 2018 study, 14- to 17-year-olds who used social media for seven hours per day were more than twice as likely to have been diagnosed with depression, received treatment from a mental health professional, or taken medication for a psychological or behavioral issue during the previous year. This was in contrast to those who used screens for only about an hour daily.

In fact, many of these researchers believe that the constant overstimulation from social networking places the nervous system in fight-or-flight mode, exacerbating disorders such as ADHD, teenage depression, oppositional defiant disorder, and teenage anxiety. However, some research on social media and teenage depression suggests that the causality is the opposite. In a study involving 600 young people, researchers discovered that social media use did not predict depressive symptoms, but more significant depressive symptoms predicted more social media use over time.

Plus, did you know that social media is the hub of bullying? That's an overstatement. Several accounts on social media are supportive and encouraging. But, according to recent statistics, 59% of American teenagers have experienced online bullying or harassment, with Instagram being the most common platform for such behavior. Cyberbullying can lead to depression in teens and may even make them more vulnerable to depression in adulthood. If you are experiencing bullying online, you need to talk about it with your parents or mentors. On the other hand, you should also consider how your online behavior may affect others and avoid posting anything that could potentially hurt someone.

Educating yourself about the dangers of interacting with strangers online is crucial. Sexual predators, scammers, identity thieves, and hackers often use social media to deceive unsuspecting users. Teens should be cautious about sharing personal information, such as their city of residence or school name, which could allow predators to find them.

Moreover, you also need to understand that online privacy is not guaranteed. When you post something online, you relinquish control over that content to anyone who sees it, and it could be shared or even turned into an embarrassing meme. As Lori Getz explains in "The Tech Savvy User's Guide to the Digital World," privacy equals control, and teens need to remember that they are giving up control of their thoughts, feelings, and images when they post them online. That sounds terrifying; the thought of someone having access to my details and private things makes me feel uncomfortable; I know it would make you feel the same way.

You might have often heard your friend argue over a post, considering whether it is fake. People on social media share their relationships, days in life, or even important events, but you rarely see anyone share their sad, hard, or heartbreaking moments. This constant exposure to one side of relationships can distort your teenage perception of relationships and how your life should be. Some of the immediate dangers of social media that can adversely affect your mental health and self-confidence are listed below:

1. Constantly Comparing

Social media plays an active role in distorting your perception of what relationships are actually like. It's not just you; even in my mid-20s, I find it hard to push by the perfect Instagram couples that do everything together and live in these giant houses. Relationships are messy and complicated and often uneventful. It's possible that their lives are not as they portray on social media, and besides, even if it is, you shouldn't be comparing them with yours. Everyone has a unique path to follow, so if yours differs, make sure you live your best time.

2. Validation & enmeshment

Social media trains teenagers to put their worth in continuous external validation. Without a strong internal validation system, you might expect relationships to fill that void and can easily become dependent and enmeshed. Since, as a teen, you are still learning how to create independent and dependent relationships, it's important to detach the need for validation and approvals from your relationships. When you dive into a relationship seeking validation, you will find yourself in a toxic cycle that will be hard to eliminate.

3. Becoming Oversexualized

Young teenagers, especially girls, quickly discover that their sexuality can be used for attention, and social media gives them a wider audience for that attention. Unfortunately, they often do not have the maturity to self-regulate. This often leads teens to base their self-worth on how they look. As a young teenage girl, you must understand that your looks are not everything you have to offer. Your intelligence and kindness also play a huge role in elevating your personality and mark on the world. This objectification can cause several severe mental health issues that are detrimental to the overall health of the teenager.

HOW CAN PARENTS HELP?

As a parent, you are responsible for monitoring your teens' social media use. However, I don't necessarily mean control over their phones and pads when I say monitor. Instead, it's important for you to teach them control and responsible use of the gadgets that they have in their use. Here are measures you can take to promote the responsible use of social media and limit its damaging effects:

Set reasonable limits.

Talk with your teen about effectively managing social media usage to prevent it from disrupting their daily activities, sleep, meals, or homework. Encourage a bedtime routine that excludes electronic media and ensure that cell phones and tablets are kept out of their bedrooms. Set an example by adhering to these rules yourself.

Monitor your teen's accounts

Let them know about your intention to regularly monitor their social media accounts, aiming to do so once a week or more. Make sure you follow through with this commitment.

Explain what's not okay.

Discourage your teen from engaging in gossip, spreading rumors, bullying, or tarnishing someone's reputation, both online and offline. Have an open conversation about what is considered appropriate and safe to share on social media.

Encourage face-to-face contact with friends.

This is particularly important for teens vulnerable to social anxiety disorder. As a parent, one can focus on allowing their children to have sleepovers or allowing them to go to the movies or have small get-togethers. This would not only ensure that they have a good time but also that they actively interact with their peers.

Talk about social media.

Start by talking about how you use social media and ask your teen about their own social media habits and how it makes them feel. Don't forget to remind them that social media often shows things that aren't realistic. Keep the conversation casual and open so you can understand their experiences better.

If you think your teen is experiencing signs or symptoms of anxiety or depression related to social media use, talk to your child's healthcare provider.

Social media has become an integral part of teenagers' communication tools and experiences during their crucial developmental period. While the negative effects of social media cannot be ignored, it's unrealistic to completely cut off your child from these online networks. Instead, a better strategy is to guide your teen to use social media as a means of boosting their self-esteem. With your guidance, social media can positively impact your child's growth and development. By teaching them how to filter out the digital noise, your teen can transform their online interactions into a valuable source of personal confidence and development.

So, since we cannot detach ourselves from social media, I have devised five ways you can avoid being addicted to it:

1. Set a time limit for your social media use
2. Find other activities to do other than social media, such as journaling, playing outdoor games, etc.
3. Don't compare yourselves to others. You are unique in your own way, embrace yourself and live a happy life.
4. Take social media breaks often to recharge and drain any toxic energy you absorb from social media.
5. Use social media for awareness and education.

Conclusively, social media has been the topic of constant criticism over the years. Everything used in moderation ensures that your positive energy is protected. You can use social media to your advantage by following body-positivity creators and mentors that can help you revive your confidence.

Teenagers today exhibit a remarkable level of social awareness and responsibility. They are well-informed about political matters, environmental issues, and each other's experiences. Utilizing social media, this generation seamlessly connects with one another, enabling them to rally around meaningful causes and drive positive progress towards a brighter future. Plus, social media has fueled several movements for equality and should be recognized for its power. While it has many downfalls, one of the most significant advantages of social media is how wide it is, in terms of knowledge, since people have access to free education on youtube and Instagram. Teenagers are exposed to several educators and coaches dispersed in diverse fields that are ready to teach them about life and academics. Social media has broadened its scope, with people offering courses to teach others about new skills that can help them flourish in their careers. Besides, it's an excellent platform for children to showcase their talents and creativity.

So, we know social media is tied to your confidence, but is there something else that can hamper your productivity? Wait to find out!

ELIMINATING PROCRASTINATION

"If you want to make an easy job seem mighty hard, just keep putting off doing it."

— OLIN MILLER

Here we are again, with amazing advice from Olin Miller. This reminds me of my time in high school. During my last years, I had a big project due for my English class. Even though I knew about this project weeks before its due date, I kept putting it off, thinking I had plenty of time to finish it. Ironically, I spent all my time doing unimportant things like surfing on social media. While these helped me recharge from my stressful days at school, I was nowhere near to finishing the project. Plus, as the deadline drew closer, I started to feel more and more stressed about the project, but I still couldn't bring myself to start working on it.

Finally, the night before the project was due, I mustered the courage to sit at my desk and start working. I stayed up late, frantically typing away at my computer and trying to finish the project before the deadline. When I finally submitted it the next day, I was exhausted and knew that the project wasn't my best work. It made me feel bad as I was not confident about the work I produced. However, somewhere I knew that I could have done better only if I had started working earlier.

Looking back, I realized my procrastination caused unnecessary stress and led to a subpar project. It taught me a valuable lesson about the importance of managing my time and staying on top of deadlines, something that Olin Miller has been hinting about all this time. But, in its most simplistic sense, what is procrastination? Why does it happen?

WHAT IS PROCRASTINATION?

As you must have probably guessed by now, procrastination is when you put off doing something important until the last minute or even after the deadline. Imagine a pressure cooker; your mom left you in charge of it and asked you to close it after 30 minutes. But, you get lost in this movie you are watching; the cooker whistles louder as the time goes above 30 minutes. By the time you reach the kitchen, half of the food in the cooker is ruined. This is exactly how procrastination works; while you are busy doing something else, what should have been your priority is ruined. Some studies define it as a failure to self-regulate, in which you put off chores despite knowing the repercussions.

Even if you're usually organized and hardworking, you've definitely spent time on unimportant things like social media or online shopping instead of performing critical jobs or school projects. Procrastination can greatly influence your career, grades, and overall quality of life, whether you're putting off a work project, homework projects, or ignoring family duties. You must be wondering what causes procrastination.While one of the factors is the foundation of this book, I want to briefly mention some of the other contributing factors of procrastination. Present bias is an important cause of procrastination. We are usually motivated by immediate rewards compared to long-term gratification, for example, watching TV instead of doing homework.

Most importantly, anyone with ADHD struggles to keep their attention in one frame since several external stimuli are inciting them. Depression and OCD are also contributing factors to the same. Nevertheless, procrastination damages your confidence.

THE LINK BETWEEN SELF-CONFIDENCE AND PROCRASTINATION

But is there a link between your low self-confidence and procrastination? It's obvious. If you read the story I shared about my English project, submitting an assignment I knew I could excel in really hurt my confidence. I did not only feel bad, but I was also upset about the fact that even though I could have done better, I didn't.

Alternatively, procrastination can ironically act as a protective measure, but in reality, it has the opposite effect. When you lack the confidence to take action, it further diminishes your confidence in yourself, creating a vicious cycle where low self-confidence and procrastination feed off each other.

Procrastination is a failure to self-regulate, making you feel like you are not in control of yourself and eroding your confidence at its core. It's like a coping strategy that undermines your ability to cope. Sounds confusing, no? For example, You were assigned a history project where you had to discuss an important historical event. However, you spent your whole week worrying about the project instead of actually researching. The time you could have spent making key notes you spent scrolling on Tiktok, now you are left with a few hours until your presentation. Since you were underprepared, you could have performed better in the presentation, which led to a decrease in your confidence. Sounds all too familiar, huh?

Think about how often you've procrastinated a task and spent the whole day worrying about it, only to find that it hardly took any time and was much easier than you expected. I'm sure it has happened to you several times.

Alternatively, self-confidence plays a crucial role when it comes to procrastination. High self-confidence means you believe in your ability to succeed at a task and approach it optimistically. On the other hand, low self-confidence means you doubt your capability to succeed. Without the expected reward of success, your emotional brain lacks the motivation to perform the task.

This thinking makes sense because why would you invest your time and energy in something if you believe you are bound to fail? But it's not true. You will succeed if you give it your 100%. This kind of negative thinking can even stop you from completing a project, even if you have confidence in certain aspects of it.

Low self-confidence also causes procrastination by acting as a protective mechanism. When you lack confidence, taking action on tasks becomes risky, as failure can further damage your self-esteem. Your subconscious mind tries to protect you from difficult tasks that can potentially deliver another devastating blow to your confidence.

Therefore, you procrastinate because you don't want to fail or fall short of your own standards, and you put off starting the task. This is especially true if you have a fixed mindset and interpret any challenge as a sign that you are not good enough. However, did you know that there are certain types of procrastinators? Sounds interesting right?

TYPES OF PROCRASTINATORS

In a study conducted by Zohar AH and her colleagues, he discovered that there are two classifications of procrastinators:

Passive procrastinators

They delay the task because they have trouble making decisions and acting on them. For example, you are struggling with a confusing chapter, so instead of practicing and revising, you put it on the back burner and ignore it until you can't.

Active procrastinators

These individuals intentionally delay tasks because they believe that working under pressure provides a sense of challenge and motivation" For example, you push your exam preparation to the last minute because you feel like you can get done more when under pressure instead of delegating time to tasks over the course of 4 weeks.

OVERTHINKER MEETS THE PROCRASTINATOR

Procrastination poses numerous interconnected dangers, where one issue caused by delaying tasks can lead to additional problems. For instance, when someone procrastinates on their schoolwork, their academic performance may suffer, leading to feelings of stress and physical deterioration. This interconnected web of consequences highlights the far-reaching impact of procrastination.

Why do we overthink things? Why do we feel the need to second-guess what is really happening with what we believe is happening? All of these questions are real-life impediments in the majority of people's lives. Sometimes we get so caught up in something that we lose sight of ourselves in the process. Most people suffer from overthinking and procrastination, leading to various problems. At some point in our lives, we all procrastinate for various reasons, whether it's because we have too many other things to do or simply because we don't want to do the task at hand. It's important not to blame ourselves excessively for procrastinating, as it's something that happens to everyone. Rather than focusing on the blame, we should acknowledge that procrastination is a common experience and ask ourselves why people procrastinate even when we lead busy lives.

HOW TO OVERCOME PROCRASTINATION

You might find yourself wondering, How can I stop procrastinating?

Fortunately, you can do several different things to fight procrastination and start getting things done on time. Consider these your procrastination exercises:

1. Make a to-do list

To help keep you on track, consider placing a due date next to each item. For example, if you have an exam, prioritize topics that you understand, revise, and finish them early. Later you can dwell and focus on complex topics.

2. Take baby steps

Break down the items on your list into small, manageable steps so your tasks don't seem so overwhelming.

3. Recognize the warning signs

Pay attention to any thoughts of procrastination and do your best to resist the urge. If you begin to think about procrastinating, force yourself to spend a few minutes working on your task.

4. Eliminate distraction

Ask yourself what pulls your attention away the most—whether it's Instagram, Facebook updates, or the local news—and turn off those sources of distraction.

5. Pat yourself on the back

When you finish an item on your to-do list on time, congratulate yourself and reward yourself by indulging in something you find fun.

Have you ever procrastinated on a task? If yes, how did you get out of the vicious cycle of laziness?

Procrastination is interlinked with low self-confidence, but it is something you can deal with strategically. It's important to remember that when you feel burned out, take time off. For me, time management has always been the key. It not only helped me manage time, but I also had time for myself. After completing the important tasks that required immediate attention, I would spare hours and indulge in doing things I loved. That's self-care, an important building block in developing your self-confidence. If you want to find out how you can take out time to do what you love, all while passing exams and meeting your deadlines, keep on reading!

7

BUILDING YOURSELF UP

"If you hear a voice within you say 'you cannot paint', then by all means paint, and that voice will be silenced."

— VINCENT VAN GOGH

Life is about taking risks and doing the impossible, or at least trying to, but I have also discovered that taking care of your body and mind is equally important. As a teenager, you are too tired to pursue what you love since all the P.E. practices and optional subjects are crushing you, or you often feel guilty for indulging in things you love. Being a teenager can be like standing on the edge of a precipice, frightening and daunting. Still, it's important to maintain a balance between doing what you love and engaging in your academic duties, such as homework, chores, and physical activity. All of this might seem a little overwhelming, and you might ask me; how do I cope with the pressure of my studies and do what I love— my answer? Self-care.

The secret of a healthy person lies in self-care. It is often ignored and overlooked by adults and teenagers, but it is a key component in regaining your self-confidence. Before we dive into all the fun ways you can indulge in self-care without feeling guilty, let's take a moment to understand what even is self-care.

THE BASICS OF SELF-CARE

So, as we divulge into the strands of self-care, I want you to remember something important– life is filled with spectacular moments that will require you to stop everything you are doing and immerse yourself in them. In those moments, try not to think about the future or the consequences of what might happen if you leave your work or assignment for a while. Anyways, let's see what self-care is.

What is Self-Care?

You might find this odd, but I call self-care 'me-time'; this is a time I have allocated for myself where I will unwind and enjoy life to its fullest. Now, the key isn't to create time but to other contributing factors such as time management, prioritization, and delegation of tasks. I already know that teenagers are drowning with assignments and deadlines during the end of 1st or 2nd term, so taking a short break can help you recharge and regain focus.

In a simple sense, to promote healthy functioning and enhance well-being, self-care is a multidimensional and multifaceted process that involves purposeful engagement in various strategies. Self-care refers to people's conscious efforts to improve their physical, mental, and emotional health. Good self-care can take many forms, such as getting enough sleep, taking breaks for fresh air, and indulging in enjoyable activities.

Me-time is essential for developing resilience towards unavoidable stressors in life. Caring for your mind and body makes you better equipped to live your best life. Unfortunately, some people consider self-care a luxury rather than a priority, resulting in feelings of overwhelm, tiredness, and inadequacy when facing life's challenges.

It's crucial to evaluate self-care practices across multiple domains to ensure holistic care of a person's mind, body, and spirit.

I always felt overwhelmed and exhausted during my last year of high school. This feeling stemmed from all the schoolwork and extracurricular activities. Despite feeling exhausted and stressed, I would continue to push myself to study and complete assignments late into the night, sacrificing my sleep and free time. Eventually, it started to take a toll on my mental health.

Until I realized that my lack of self-care was affecting my physical and mental health adversely. I decided to make some changes and prioritize self-care. I began to set a bedtime for myself, aiming to get at least 8 hours of sleep each night. I also started taking regular breaks from studying to engage in activities I enjoyed, such as playing music and sports.

As I began incorporating self-care into my routine, I noticed a significant improvement in my mood and energy levels. In fact, I felt more focused and productive during my study sessions and could enjoy my free time without feeling guilty or stressed. By prioritizing self-care, I was able to achieve a better balance in my life and maintain my physical, mental, and emotional health.

Do you see the power of self-care? Let me tell you why it's essential as well.

Throughout the ambit of research and literature reviews, having an effective self-care routine has been shown to have many important health benefits. Some of these include:

- Reducing anxiety and depression
- Reducing stress and improving resilience
- Improving happiness
- Increasing energy
- Reducing burnout
- Stronger interpersonal relationships

Moreover, as per the World Health Organization (WHO), self-care is crucial because it plays a vital role in promoting health, preventing diseases, and supporting individuals in various ways. In fact, specific forms of self-care can be linked to different health benefits. For example, physical activity, sleep, etc., are all connected to an increased lifetime.

Types of Self-Care

Interestingly, did you know that there were different types of self-care? This ensures that when you make a self-care plan, it is well constructed as you know what you need–

Self-care isn't just about finding ways to relax. It's about caring for yourself mentally, physically, emotionally, socially, and spiritually. To care for your health and well-being, finding a balance that allows you to address each of these areas is important. At times, you may need more self-care in a specific area to restore balance and find relief from a stressor in your life. Here are five areas that would require your immediate attention when it comes to self-care:

1. Physical Self-Care

If you want your body to function properly, you must take care of it. Remember that there is a strong link between your body and your thoughts. You'll think and feel better if you take care of your body.

2. Social Self-Care

Having a social life is crucial for self-care, but it can be challenging to prioritize friendships and relationships when life gets busy. Establishing intimate relationships with people is essential for one's general well-being, and the most effective method to do so is to invest time and effort in developing and sustaining those relationships.

3. Mental Self-Care

How you think and the things you fill your head with massively impact your psychological well-being.

Mental self-care involves activities that keep your mind sharp, such as puzzles or learning about a topic that interests you. Watching movies or reading books that inspire you may help to energize your thoughts. Doing tasks that assist you in staying mentally well is also part of mental self-care. Self-compassion and acceptance, for example, can assist you in maintaining a healthier inner dialogue.

4. Spiritual Self-Care

Research indicates that a lifestyle incorporating religion or spirituality tends to be healthier overall. Nevertheless, nurturing your spirit doesn't necessarily have to be tied to religion. It can encompass anything that enables you to foster a more profound meaning, understanding, or connection with the universe.

5. Emotional Self-Care

Having healthy coping skills to manage uncomfortable emotions such as anger, anxiety, and sadness is essential. Emotional self-care involves engaging in activities that allow you to acknowledge and express your feelings regularly and safely.

Whether you talk to a parent or close friend about how you feel or set aside time for leisure activities that help you process your emotions, it's important to incorporate emotional self-care into your life.

Unfortunately, you will experience barriers when it comes to completely achieving your self-care routine. But don't worry, I will teach you how to surpass them. However, before we do that, It's important for you to be aware of these barriers.

Medical Barriers

Research shows these basic self-care practices can prevent 60 to 70 percent of chronic diseases. However, many people need to discuss self-care with their doctors, and physicians often need more time or training to address behavioral changes with patients. To incorporate self-care into doctor visits, you should take responsibility for bringing up self-care with your doctors and consider scheduling an integrative health or lifestyle visit. Writing down questions before the visit can also help ensure that self-care concerns are addressed.

Personal Barriers

According to the Harris Poll, consumers don't prioritize self-care because many think it requires either enough time or money. However, self-care doesn't have to be a separate activity; it can be integrated into daily routines. Many people believe self-care is selfish, especially women and young girls who are often told to prioritize others before themselves. But neglecting self-care can actually be a selfish action as it depletes us and hinders our ability to care for others. While organic foods may be expensive, the long-term consequences of not caring for ourselves could be even more costly. Don't avoid indulging in things you like, even if it incites criticism from people.

STRATEGIES TO IMPROVE SELF-CARE

Self-care might seem challenging to incorporate into your life. However, it is crucial for you to reclaim the things and hobbies you like in order to boost your confidence. Here are some strategies that I used to introduce self-care habits into my lifestyle:

1. Good News Bestie

We all have a friend that we call when we are sad or happy. To boost confidence, find a friend you can celebrate your successes with. When you appreciate little moments, they become special. Celebrate each other and support your goals.

2. Forgiveness

Any pent-up anger in your heart immensely impacts your soul and mind. Be sure to forgive yourself; place your hand on your heart, close your eyes, and repeat, 'I am sorry for being so hard on you. You are amazing.' Give yourself a little bit of credit for pulling out of your darkest moments.

3. A List of Things You Love About Yourself

This is an easy hit. Do you remember a few years ago, the 'TBH' (To be honest) trend was rampant on Facebook? Be honest to yourself and list 5-6 things you love about yourself. This way, you will see things in a different light.

ACCEPTANCE AND LOVE

Self-love

Self-love involves valuing oneself and nurturing personal growth through activities that support physical, psychological, and spiritual well-being. It is the act of prioritizing one's happiness and well-being and not compromising it to please others. It also means refusing to accept less than what one deserves.

Now that you understand what self-love means, it's important to note that it drives individuals to make healthy life choices. There are various methods to practice self-love, including becoming mindful and aware of one's thoughts, feelings, and desires. One should prioritize fulfilling their needs rather than wanting to steer clear of destructive behavior patterns and increase self-love. Additionally, taking good care of oneself, such as practicing healthy habits, is essential to self-love.

Self-acceptance

I have a question for you to think about– Do you accept yourself? The mistakes you make and the flaws that you see in yourself?

Accepting yourself means acknowledging and embracing all of your qualities, including the positive and negative ones, as well as your physical and mental characteristics.

Practicing self-acceptance and self-care daily can gradually increase your level of self-acceptance over time. You can accept yourself gracefully in several ways, such as practicing gratitude, reframing negative thoughts, choosing a positive support system, meditating, and forgiving yourself for past mistakes (Waters, 2021). For example, during your journey to achieving self-confidence, you relied on your best friend for comfort and support. Throughout this process, they helped you spread kindness and reaffirm positivity in your life.

This shows that they became a positive support system, which is a crucial element in your journey.

By writing down negative beliefs and reframing them with positive self-talk, practicing gratitude, and spending time with positive people, you can improve your self-image and reduce self-criticism. Meditation can help detach from negative self-talk, promoting inner peace and psychological well-being. Forgiveness is an essential step towards self-acceptance and can be achieved by identifying judgments and writing them down.

Self-awareness

Self-awareness is your ability to perceive and understand what makes you who you are, including your personality, actions, values, beliefs, emotions, and thoughts. Essentially, it is a psychological state in which the self becomes the focus of attention (Cherry, 2023).

To improve your self-awareness, there are various practices you can engage in, such as meditation, journaling, talk therapy, and developing emotional intelligence. Meditation is particularly beneficial because it allows you to observe your thoughts and feelings without the need to change them. Journaling helps you reflect on your thoughts, behaviors, and areas needing improvement, while talk therapy like CBT can help you identify and address negative thought patterns. You can improve your self-awareness and emotional intelligence by practicing healthy emotional expression and active listening.

Final Word...

All in all, self-care is an integral part of your overall healthcare because it enables you to do things you love. Life is about finding joy in the little things we stumble upon during the day. Being more accepting, loving, and kind towards yourself is crucial. As human beings, we lift heavy burdens and pull ourselves through great ordeals; it is only fair that we indulge in things that make us happy once in a while. However, the puzzle of self-care and confidence is incomplete without a supporting element. Do you know what it is? If this is inciting your curiosity, move to the next chapter and find out what completes the package of self-care and self-confidence.

8

MINDING YOUR THOUGHTS

"When virtues are pointed out first, flaws seem less insurmountable."

— JUDITH MARTIN

By now, you're probably familiar with the term' negative self-talk'. It's been a popular topic amongst many lifestyle YouTubers and podcast creators. But, if you haven't heard of negative self-talk like me, you are in for a wild ride. This is undoubtedly something we humans indulge in often. Negative self-talk can take many forms, from appearing reasonable and cautious to being harsh and judgmental. It might begin with a rational examination of a situation but quickly devolve into irrational and fear-based ideas. This type of negative self-talk may match previous comments from a parent or friend and may include cognitive distortions such as catastrophizing and blaming. Negative self-talk is defined as any inner dialogue that inhibits your conviction in your abilities and potential and impedes good improvements in your life. As a result, it generates tension and can hamper your achievement. In fact, negative self-talk can become destructive when it starts happening regularly.

Let me give you some perspective—

After receiving his final term results, Andy became instantaneously depressed because of poor grades and low performance. He decided to drop his favorite subject, mathematics, since he flunked the subject. Every day of the summer break, Andy would convince himself that he was not cut out to major in mathematics in his college. 'I can't do it' or 'I am a failure' would be among the few conversations he would have with himself.

Every time he would try to attempt a math problem given to him as summer break homework, he would have a panic attack. A little voice in the back of his mind told him that he couldn't do it. It jumbled his mind and would often cause him to lose focus. Eventually, he shared this problem with his father, who gave him a piece of wonderful advice: 'You are not a failure, Andy. Your mind is playing a trick on you. Always remember when you are at war with yourself, close your eyes, and remind yourself about all your successes. Your achievements are proof that you are a smart person. Besides, failures are a part of life.'

By the time school started again, Andy was ready to face math again. He revised all the concepts and gave his exams proactively. Despite his inner critic discouraging him, he made sure that every time he had a negative thought, he would rummage through his mind for a positive anchor.

This shows that having a mechanism that triggers your positive thoughts can help you overcome any negative conversation your mind is indulging in and boost your confidence.

CAUSES OF NEGATIVE SELF TALK

Negative self-talk often originates from feelings of depression, low self-confidence, and anxiety, and it can also be indicative of a more significant mental health issue. However, some habits can trigger negative self-talk. These habits include:

Not addressing relationship problems

Having dysfunctional families, toxic friends, or bad teachers can cause you to experience stress. Avoiding direct communication to address relationship issues can accumulate stress, frustration, and resentment, resulting in a hostile relationship environment (Hui, 2021). Such negativity can create harmful patterns of thinking that may exacerbate the conflict and worsen the relationship, such as friendships or your relationship with your parents.

Poor health habits

You will not feel good mentally if you don't feel good physically. Having bad physical health automatically leads to low self-confidence and bad mental health (Hui, 2021). When you repeatedly expose yourself to negative thoughts in certain areas, your mind will start to accept them as true, and you will believe that we deserve them. On the other hand, adopting a healthy lifestyle that suits your individual needs can positively impact your mental well-being.

Too much time alone

Human beings must mingle and socialize. We are called social animals for a reason, right? If you are not cautious, negative self-talk can intensify when you experience social isolation or spend excessive amounts of time alone (Hui, 2021). The absence of other people to divert your attention from negative thoughts is the underlying reason for this phenomenon (Taylor, 2018).

Not asking for help

To alleviate negative self-talk, seeking help can be a significant step. Nevertheless, if you have a tendency to refrain from seeking help when required, this behavior may worsen your negative self-talk.

Failing to practice self-care

Again, as you explored in the previous chapter, self-care is integral to your life. A habit of pushing emotions down may end up making you feel even worse. Make sure to pick up a hobby that you like and enjoy.

Surrounding yourself with negative people

Do you remember our discussion about the toxic environment in the previous chapters? Similarly, negative people can induce negative thoughts in your mind. It's important to stay clear of such people. Regularly indulging in any of the mentioned habits can lead to negative self-talk.

CONSEQUENCES OF NEGATIVE SELF TALK

Everyone is fighting their own battle, but it all happens so quietly that you are forced to believe that only you feel this way. That's not true; you are not alone. Therefore it is vital for you to ask for help.

Negative self-talk can hinder your capacity to achieve your greatest potential and become your best self. Although negative self-talk is a natural part of human life, it heightens when you embark on the journey of growth (Taylor, 2018). While research demonstrates that positive self-talk can improve mood, productivity, and self-esteem, negative self-talk can damage emotional well-being, undermine self-confidence, and lead to self-blame (Bailen, 2018).

Everything seems impossible to attain or further away from your reach. It's only because you are trying to do multiple things simultaneously. No one can achieve that; it's impossible. Your mind is immersed in negative self-talk, which hinders your positivity (Taylor, 2018). As you strive to strike a balance between pursuing a subject you desire or need and living the life you imagined, you don't just feel bad about disappointing your parents, teachers, or friends; you also feel guilty about practicing self-care (Scott, 2022). Plus, the guilt of not living up to your parent's expectations or embarrassment about telling a friend how stressed you are is crushing you. It's almost as if you can never make time for yourself without feeling guilty. But that is far from the truth. Here are some obvious consequences of negative self-talk:

1. Limited thinking

The more you tell yourself that you can't do something, the more likely you will fail at it (Scott, 2022).

2. Perfectionism

The belief that perfection is achievable can lead one to devalue excellence and regard anything less than perfection as inadequate (Scott, 2022). On the other hand, individuals who strive for high achievement but do not obsess over attaining perfection tend to fare better. They experience less stress and are content with their accomplishments without over-analyzing them for potential areas of improvement.

3. Feelings of depression

Some research has shown that negative self-talk can lead to a worsening of feelings of depression. If left unchecked, this could be pretty damaging (Scott, 2022).

4. Low self-esteem

When you negatively talk with yourself, demotivate and discourage yourself consistently, you hinder opportunities and your personal growth. This low self-esteem causes you to have social anxiety and disconnect from people.

Ironically, your mind disrupts your confidence. Your consciousness constantly hits you with 'You are not good enough' or 'You can't do this.' Comments like these can hurt your self-confidence immensely (Morin, 2022). This sets the alarm in your mind that you are doing something wrong when you are only trying to thrive. It's natural for teenagers to experience self-doubt and negative thoughts, but with time, they can recover more quickly, and the guilt won't be as intense (Scott, 2022).

But you must confront the negativity within your mind, change your perspective and detach from the cycle of self-doubt if you want to overcome and strive to be your best. There are several ways you can deal with negative thoughts. But before diving into that, did you know there are different types of negative self-talk? I know, right! It's interesting.

TYPES OF NEGATIVE SELF-TALK

There are different types of negative self-talk that we indulge in frequently. Some common types of negative self-talk are:

Filtering

Negative filtering means you filter out all the positive information about a specific event and only allow the negative parts to wander in your mind. In other words, negative filtering magnifies negative aspects while disregarding the positive. After a successful day at school, you focus solely on what could have been accomplished rather than how much fun you had (Scott, 2022).

Personalizing

When something bad occurs, you automatically blame yourself. Catastrophizing. You automatically anticipate the worst without facts that the worse will happen (Scott, 2022). The test you prepared so hard for didn't go well, and then you think the rest of your day will be a disaster.

Blaming

Instead of taking responsibility for your thoughts and feelings, you might try to place the blame on someone else for what happened to you.

Magnifying

You make a big deal out of minor problems. For example, you got a 70 on a test instead of a 90. It's okay to settle for a 70 and work harder next time.

Perfectionism

Keeping impossible standards and trying to be more perfect sets you up for failure. You either get a 20/20 on your exam, or it's a failed attempt. This thinking is problematic because you put yourself under unrealistic expectations (Morin, 2022).

Polarizing

You see things only as either good or bad. There is no middle ground (Scott, 2022).

I can already place myself under some of these headings, can you?

SILENCE THE CRITIC

Nevertheless, if you are someone that struggles with your inner critic, here are 7 ways to silence that little voice inside your head that triggers you and lowers your self-confidence:

1. Develop an awareness of your thoughts

We are often unaware of the messages we send ourselves because we are accustomed to our own narrations. It is critical to be aware of our thoughts and recognize that they are not always correct. Our perceptions are frequently inflated, biased, and disproportionate (Hunt, 2021).

2. Stop ruminating

If you make a mistake or have a bad day, you may feel compelled to replay the events in your mind. This, however, will not help you fix the problem and may make you feel worse (Hunt, 2021). Instead of avoiding thinking about it, which might lead to additional attention on the negative thoughts, distract yourself with an activity such as going for a walk, organizing your desk, or chatting about anything else. This will help you stop ruminating and stop having critical thoughts.

3. Ask yourself what advice you'd give to a friend

It's unlikely that you would say things like "You're so stupid" or "You can't do anything right" to a friend who expressed feelings of self-doubt. However, we tend to be harsher on ourselves and say those things to ourselves. It would be more compassionate to offer words of encouragement to ourselves, such as "It's okay to make mistakes" or "This one bad day doesn't define you. (Hunt, 2021)" We should treat ourselves with the same kindness we would treat a friend and apply those encouraging words to our own lives.

4. Examine the evidence

You need to recognize when your negative thoughts have become excessively negative. So, reverse your perception; instead of saying, "I'll never be able to pass these exams," you can say, 'I'll give my 100% to this test'. In fact, it can be beneficial to write things down at times. Make a line along the center of a piece of paper (Hunt, 2021). List all of the evidence that supports your point of view on one side. On the other hand, list all the evidence to the contrary.

5. Replace overly critical thoughts with more accurate statements

Convert an overly despairing thought into a more rational and realistic statement. When you catch yourself thinking, "I never do anything right," replace it with a balanced statement like, "It's okay for me to not be great at everything." (Hunt, 2021) Respond with a more accurate statement each time you think an exaggeratedly negative thought. We have more control over our thoughts than we are led to believe. There's a split second before an intrusive thought enters where we can replace it with a more optimistic one.

6. Consider how bad it would be if your thoughts were true

Sometimes, we may be inclined to imagine a minor mistake spiraling into a major disaster. However, in reality, the outcome of a worst-case scenario may not be as dire as we anticipate (Hunt, 2021). To illustrate, consider the scenario where you anticipate embarrassment during a presentation. Recognizing your ability to manage difficulties and setbacks can enhance your self-assurance and minimize persistent anxious thoughts (Hunt, 2021).

7. Balance acceptance with self-improvement

There's a difference between constantly telling yourself you're not good enough and reminding yourself that you can improve. Accept your imperfections as they are, but resign yourself to working on the issues you want to fix. Although it may appear counterintuitive, you can do both (Hunt, 2021).

Accept that you are anxious in social circumstances but also decide to get more comfortable with public speaking. Accepting your flaws for what they are now does not imply that you must remain that way. Recognize your weaknesses while staying motivated to be a work in progress as you attempt to improve.

SHIFTING THE ENERGIES

This is a love letter to positive self-talk. It has changed my life for the better, and it can do the same for you. It might sound funny, but believe me, it works. You reconfigure your mind into believing that you are capable and strong; that is when you truly channel your worth and resilience.

When it comes to our skills and talent, we all have moments of self-doubt. Yet, suppose you continuously contemplate whether you're good or capable enough to do what you want. Henceforth the negativity bias indicates that you have a tendency to focus on what you did "wrong" rather than what you did right. Sounds familiar?

For example, during my finals after an exam, I constantly worry about what I did wrong and right. It was as if my life revolved around the mistakes I made in that paper. I was too afraid to even take the review classes where my teachers would review the paper. Eventually, I realized that this was an exhausting chain of thought. When I decided to change my thought process, it felt like an elephant's leg was off my chest, and during the exam season, I could finally breathe.

Consider a time when you did something but were preoccupied with the one thing you could have done better. Although 90% of your efforts were successful, you ponder about the other 10% that may have been better. When you are overly critical of that small percentage and continuously doubt your work and talents, your negative self-talk manifests as self-doubt and therefore lowers your confidence.

Okay, I know it's easier said than done but hear me out. It took me years to manifest and master the art of negating negative bias. But before we jump into what you can do to prevent it, it's important to revisit the devastating impact of negative self-talk. Negative self-talk not only decreases your confidence but also invades your perspective on life and challenges. Eventually, you are unable to manage stress strategically and crumble in the face of any incident. It shakes your ability to face the realities and adversaries of life because you don't believe in yourself. Challenging negative beliefs involves reframing your negative mindset to incorporate a positive shift in it. But, as we know, contesting these thoughts requires a little more effort than we would care to admit.

So, what can you do to prevent this?

Well, for starters, consider your efforts instead of the outcome. This sounds a little tricky, but in a research from 2019, it was found that children who make it a habit of indulging in 'effort talk' did way better in mathematics compared to children who only practiced positive talk (Mayo Clinic, 2019). Therefore, by prioritizing their efforts over the outcome, participants who made use of effort talk could readily detach themselves from the persona of a negative mindset about their abilities and talent. When you reframe your mindset, you can buffer out any negative conjecture holding you back from achieving your true potential. An excellent way to eliminate a bad habit is to replace it with a good one. Here are 3 steps to incorporate positive self-talk:

1. Start with noticing your thoughts and listen to what you are telling yourself.

2. Start to challenge your negative thoughts by asking yourself questions like:

- Am I being overly critical of myself?

- Would I say this to a friend?
- Am I overreacting?
- Is it really only good or bad? Is there any middle ground? Is this thought even true? Is there actual proof or evidence for what I am thinking?
- Am I making any assumptions? Can I really know what other people are thinking or feeling?
- Can I change this situation?

3. Start practicing reframing your thoughts by using more positive words and phrasing (Mayo Clinic, 2019).

REBUILD YOUR CONFIDENCE

As a teenager, I often felt trapped in an ally with unwanted thoughts. So, it is important for you to steer clear of unwanted thoughts. Building self-confidence through skills and experience can be a gradual process, but here are some steps you can take to help boost your self-confidence:

1. What are your strengths

Take time to reflect on what you are good at and what skills you have developed. Write them down and remind yourself of them regularly.

2. Set achievable goals

Set realistic goals that are challenging but achievable. As you reach each goal, you will gain confidence in your abilities.

3. Step out of your comfort zone

Try new things and take on challenges that push you out of your comfort zone. This will help you develop new skills and gain experience, which will, in turn, increase your self-confidence.

4. Practice, practice, practice

The more you practice a skill, the better you will become at it. Set aside time to practice your skills regularly, whether through a hobby, a sport, or a work-related task.

5. Accept mistakes and learn from them

Nobody is perfect, and mistakes are a natural part of the learning process. Accept your mistakes and use them as an opportunity to learn and grow (Mayo Clinic, 2019).

6. Celebrate your successes

Celebrate your successes, no matter how small they may seem. Acknowledge your accomplishments and give yourself credit for your hard work and achievements.

7. Develop your sense of self

Practicing self-awareness can be a powerful tool in identifying your strong identity. Ask yourself some difficult questions such as– Who am I? What do I enjoy? It's important that you have a value system. People might criticize your actions and perception, but it won't affect you if you truly value what you believe (Morin, 2022). When you have a strong sense of self, you are able to add a building block to your ladder of confidence. Be confident in who you are and what you stand for. You will find that your confidence will increase, and so will your willingness to ignore haters.

8. Surround yourself with supportive people

Friends and family members who are continuously judgmental might significantly negatively impact your mental health. Knowing that someone you care about has bad feelings about you is really upsetting. Relationships with people who accept your genuine self and are supportive and willing to talk about it - even if they can sometimes be a little "judgy" - are critical for preserving mental health.

9. Take back control

You must take back control of your own feelings. You cannot control how people perceive you. Consider practicing mindful techniques such as meditation, yoga, and breathing techniques to accept how you feel in the moment and be aware of them. Plus, learning to be in the moment can help you steer away from unwanted thoughts.

So, to sum it up, building self-confidence is a process that takes time and effort. By setting achievable goals, focusing on your strengths, stepping out of your comfort zone, practicing your skills, learning from mistakes, seeking feedback, and celebrating your successes, you can gradually build self-confidence and feel more confident in your abilities. Like you explored throughout this chapter, reframing your negative thoughts is another effective way to manage guilt and self-doubt. Plus, manage your time and avoid procrastinating. For that, make a thoughtful schedule to ensure that you dedicate quality time to your family while also being productive throughout your school week.

Time management enables you to balance your school time with the things you love to do. Besides, it also ensures that you have time for self-care. With a managed timetable, you can finish prioritized tasks and later spend time with your friends or even dedicate an hour to indulging in your hobbies. Additionally, it is important to ask for help when you need it. Ask for the support of your family members or close friends to help with schoolwork and responsibilities. Also, take the time to commit to a self-care routine. Set aside time for things that bring you joy and relaxation.

Now, you know how to deal with your negative thoughts. I want to redirect your attention toward caring for yourself; you are your best friend. Try to have healthy conversations with yourself that involve self-love. During my twenties, I have learned the importance of acceptance, so don't be afraid to take a break from your life and appreciate help from people when needed. Remember to give yourself grace and acknowledge that you are doing the best you can, whether it's studying for your exam or preparing for a retake. It's equally important to note that you have the power to detach and scrape the negativity out of your life. When you shut your doors to the useless banter, your life seems more peaceful.

POSITIVE AFFIRMATIONS

Positive affirmations give you an optimistic view of life. You are able to accept and love yourself in many ways. Here are 20 affirmations that you can rely on when feeling down: (*Positive Self Talk: What It Is and Why It's Important? - Conflict Center*, n.d.)

- "I am enough."
- "Look at me go! I can do it all."
- "I love myself."
- "I forgive myself."
- "I let go and I am free."
- "I am doing the best I can and that is enough."
- "I release the past and embrace the present."
- "Wherever I go, I am well."
- "I can handle whatever comes my way."
- "I am safe and protected."
- "I am safe and in control."
- "I have done this before, and I can do it again."
- "This too shall pass."
- "I am strong."
- "I trust myself."
- "I am capable.
- "I act with confidence because I know what I am doing."
- "I am different and unique, and that is okay."
- "I am safe in the company of others."
- "I love and I am loved."
- "I am prepared and ready for this situation." (Crumpler, 2022)

That said, negative self-talk can be countered by positive affirmations and a healthy balance between what you think about yourself and what others perceive about you. Remember, you are wonderful, and the best way to regain confidence is to believe that you are capable of great things in this world. So you must find your strengths and improve them respectively. If you want to know how to do that, keep on reading.

BUILDING YOURSELF FROM WITHIN

"The very best thing you can do for the whole world is to make the most of yourself."

— WALLACE WATTLES

Wallace Wattles was a new thought writer known for his positive thinking and self-help books. What he truly means by 'make the most out of yourself' is refurbishing your skills and using them to their fullest. This signifies the importance of using our inner strength to pursue life. A society that fixates on flaws and urges people to constantly find new ways to improve their appearances consequently overshadows their strengths. Especially the hustle culture, which has now become an evident trend, constantly burdens young people to learn new skills, distracting them from focusing on what they already know. Besides, all of this causes teenagers to be evidently hard on themselves and makes it difficult for them to identify their strengths.

It might take some time for you to shift your focus from the flaws that you carry to the strengths that you have, but when you do, I promise you won't want to go back. When you see your best traits and natural talents in a positive light, you give yourself the best chance of reaching your full potential. Let me share an experience with you—

Alex and I took biology together, and he was an intelligent kid. But, he would often feel lost in the crowd. Often he felt like he had no talents or strengths, which caused chaos in his life's rhythms. So, during the talent show auditioning, I encouraged him to participate. He was hesitant at first, but with some encouragement, he decided to try it. He had never sung in front of anyone before, but he had always enjoyed singing to himself. On the day of the talent show, Alex nervously walked onto the stage and began to sing. As he sang, he felt a sense of liberation and joy that he had never experienced before. He felt he was meant to be on stage and share his voice with others. After the talent show, Alex received so much positive feedback and encouragement from his friends and classmates. They told him that he had an amazing voice and should pursue singing. Alex was shocked. That was merely the beginning. He went on to pursue other strengths that were hidden inside of him. So, do you see the power your inner strength wields?

OVERVIEW OF INNER STRENGTH

Do you remember self-awareness from the previous chapters? Likewise, self-awareness and perception are crucial factors in elevating your performance. You need to be aware of the value you add to whatever you are pursuing. Acknowledging your strengths is a plausible way of giving your mind and creativity the room to embark on a successful journey of becoming better versions (Griggs, 2023).

Using inner strength requires contentment, consideration, calmness, patience, and endurance to sustain such restraint throughout life (Araya, 2023). Inner strength is essential to living your dream life, as it helps you face obstacles with resilience and perseverance.

If you keep up with the Marvel and D.C. universe, Captain America is a character well-known for resilience and strength. He stood against the grain and accepted the consequences, but his inner strength brought him peace with every decision he made (Rebecca, 2019). His story is leveled on mustering courage and finding your will to push through even in the darkest moments of your life.

Compassion and thoughtful action are forms of inner strength when handling life's challenges, whether going against popular opinion or confronting indifference. Understanding and using your inner strength is crucial to achieving success and happiness. Therefore it is important for you to start building your inner strength. Here are 5 ways you can rebuild your courage (use them wisely):

1. Turn your 'shoulds' into 'musts'

People often cannot achieve their dreams because they lack focus and concentration (Griggs, 2023). Many people only dabble and never commit to mastering a particular goal. To live the desired life, every step towards that goal must be a "must" - an essential action that cannot be neglected.

2. Let go of the past

If you live in the past, it is merely your future. Nobody has succeeded. Everyone has had difficulties and setbacks (Griggs, 2023). The ability to identify the lesson in failure, attribute a positive meaning to it, and then get back up and keep going separates those who eventually become successful from those who give up (Araya, 2023). Stop telling yourself disempowering stories about your mistakes and failures in the past. Change your mental script to only enable good thoughts.

3. Focus and Focus

This is possibly the most significant. The best way to put it is as 'where focus goes, energy flows,' and if you focus on your long-term goals, the sky's the limit. Don't obsess about what has gone wrong or what could go wrong (Araya, 2023). Remember that there is only one moment. The past is gone, and the future exists only in your mind. Make the decision now to concentrate on what really matters: reaching your objectives. When you have a single-minded goal, your failures and negative experiences seem minor and inconsequential.

4. Examine previous experiences

Your life experiences are invaluable instruments for developing inner strength. When you're struggling to discover inner strength, consider this: What belief or sensation (such as self-confidence or enthusiasm) might simplify obtaining inner strength right now? Have I felt this way more (or less) in the past, and what has changed since then? Everything becomes a resource when you learn from previous experiences (Araya, 2023).

5. Set yourself up for success

To develop your inner strength, ask what is not enough. You need to prepare yourself to discover the strength you want by establishing a routine and a positive mindset and focusing on your strengths to achieve your goals (Araya, 2023).

So, finding your inner strength is impeccable in how you perceive yourself and approach life's difficulties.

GROWTH MINDSET

During your teenage years, your brain undergoes a remodeling experience which helps you have a stronger and more effective brain. You must have heard the phrase 'as you grow, you mature' if not directly or indirectly linked to your brain's bandwidth. Unfortunately, this remodeling process involves periods of intense emotional reactions, risk-taking behavior, boundary-pushing, and inconsistent impulse control. When we are younger, we only see the world from a singular face, but as we grow, we are able to see things in a more abstract way (Schwarz, 2022). As a teenager, you are able to be more creative with your problem-solving and think critically about yourself and others. Thus, you are trying to find yourself. Therefore, during this period, it is increasingly important for you to build strong, healthy, "growth mindset" brains.

Now, you must be wondering– what even is a growth mindset? A growth mindset involves believing that people can develop and enhance their abilities, whereas a "fixed mindset" revolves around the belief that intelligence and capabilities are innate and cannot change significantly.

Many teens are stuck in a fixed mindset. They believe they are "not good at math" or "I will never be on the tennis team (Schwarz, 2022)."

- Improve their results ("Meeting with my algebra tutor helped me understand the last unit")
- Develop talents ("I enjoy signing and I can get better with practice")
- Grow their skills ("Practicing daily will improve my serve") (Schwarz, 2022).

The benefits of a growth mindset don't stop at grades and athletics; in fact, it can be applied to anything you are passionate about, strengthening your friendships, enhancing your relationships, gaining recognition as a valuable team member, voicing your beliefs, or conquering a fear. Thus, ensure that you have a space to think, process, and even question the status quo. Find outlets for your creativity, allow yourself to see appropriate alternatives to risky behavior, and try practicing setting goals. Here are 4 ways you can improve your growth mindset and reach your full potential:

1. Foster Grit

According to Dr. Angela Lee Duckworth, grit - a combination of passion and perseverance toward long-term goals - strongly predicts academic and professional success (Schwarz, 2022). Motivate yourself to keep going and working hard towards your goals, as grit will set you apart and help you achieve success.

2. Praise Pliable Efforts

Praising your efforts or even acknowledging them can help you foster a growth mindset. You can regain confidence and encourage repeated behavior by recognizing your persistence, hard work, ambition, determination, and progress (Schwarz, 2022).

3. Write Down Ambitions, Goals, Dreams

We all have dreams and goals, and so do teens. In fact, they are overflowing the ambitions, goals, and dreams, but they need pre-planning to achieve them. Experts suggest writing down goals, as even audacious ones have a serious chance of success. A study found people who write goals down are 42% more likely to achieve them, making dreams concrete and keeping them motivated (Schwarz, 2022). So, make a mind map and write down all your plans.

4. Take on Challenges

During the teenage years, low self-confidence can make taking risks difficult. But shattering negative self-talk and finding the courage to take on challenges, even if failure is possible, is essential. Let's take advice from the queen of confidence; taylor swift herself

"To me, fearlessness is not the absence of fear. To me, fearless is living in spite of those things that scare you to death,"

5. Focus on the Journey, Not the Destination

Teenagers often focus on the final destination, influenced by social media, peers, and culture. However, the progress they make each day holds life's valuable lessons, and their journey is where transformations occur. By being appreciative and mindful of their progress, teens can learn to love the process of life, including the ups, downs, challenges, and triumphs. Instead of fixating on the destination, appreciate where you are, how far you've come, and where you're headed. The journey is where the magic happens. (Schwarz, 2022)

Final Word…

In a nutshell, having a growth mindset enables you to explore your strengths and further your capabilities. Besides, you will be able to identify your strengths and focus on them, improve them, and later rely on them when you are older. But, for that to happen, you need to create a safe space within your mind. If you are interested in creating a calm and gentle space where you can unwind and let your creativity flow, flip the page!

10

BREAKING A SWEAT

"He who has health has hope and he who has hope has everything."

— ARABIAN PROVERB

Your body is interconnected with your soul and mind, so every time your mind is distressed, your body feels the pressure more closely than you can imagine. During my high school years, I was an active participant in most of the sports that were offered. The practices and match preparations installed two important elements in me; first, I was taught discipline throughout my practices. Second, the time I spent working out or preparing myself for any competition helped me detach myself from all the academic pressure. Sports became my time off, giving my body purpose and mind direction. While working out, my mind focused on engaging my body in high-intensity training, after which I felt happier, as if I had accomplished something big.

Now, I know some of you are really enthusiastic about sports, and you should be. I learned about the importance of sports later in my twenties when I started working out regularly. It has become my way of releasing all the tension and stress from my body. In fact, I would go as far as to call it 'therapeutic' for me.

Your mind and body have an indisputable connection that you must reintegrate to boost your self-confidence. Let's be honest; when we are healers, we feel much better about ourselves and our lives. But did you know that exercising, or any physical activity for that matter, can improve your mental health?

BENEFITS OF EXERCISE

Anxiety can take a toll on a person's mental health, increasing their risk for other psychiatric disorders such as depression and contributing to health issues like cardiovascular problems. Have you ever felt like the world's weight is too burdensome for you to carry? Or that your mind is going at 100mph when you go to bed?

Interestingly, a study has shown that people with anxiety tend to be less physically active and engage in less intense forms of physical activity, if any at all. This is ironic because engaging in physical activity, like putting on your sneakers and running, is one of the best non-medical solutions for preventing and treating anxiety. Recently, I landed on this research by the National College Health Association, where they concluded that 63% of students experience high anxiety levels during their first year in college or school. Now, I understand that you must be afraid and nervous to go to school and meet all these new people, so I have a trick to release all that anxiety. Yes, you have guessed it right, it's exercise. Don't get me wrong, I am not expecting you to make and maintain a 6-days-a-week, 1-hour workout regimen; instead, I want you to pick a physical activity you love, like running, walking, or playing sports. Afterward, I want you to take 30 mins and indulge in that activity. This can be your short me-time where you engage in something you love, but it makes you sweat.

What are the benefits of exercising?

Exercise can help you manage anxiety since it diverts your attention from the cause of your worries. You can ease muscle tension, which contributes to feelings of anxiety, by exercising your body. Exercise also improves brain chemistry by raising concentrations of key anti-anxiety neurochemicals such as serotonin, GABA, BDNF, and endocannabinoids. The executive function-related frontal regions of the brain are activated along with this change in brain chemistry, which can assist in controlling the amygdala, our brain's warning system. Additionally, regular exercise can help us develop the necessary resources to withstand powerful emotions. Again, there is evidence that exercise positively affects your mental health. Here are the most common benefits that research supports:

1. Can relieve stress

Regular exercise is marketed as a powerful stress reliever, which may come as no surprise to you.

You may have experienced this firsthand or may not, but exercise truly affects your mind and body. For instance, you might have made the decision to go to the gym after a particularly stressful day at work and felt a little relaxation when you got home (Ratey, 2019).

Exercise is known to alleviate stress by lowering levels of stress-related chemicals like cortisol and adrenaline.

2. May improve self-confidence

Having improved positive self-image and self-confidence are two additional factors that exercise has on mental health.

According to multiple studies, regular exercise can help people feel better about themselves and their bodies. Therefore, exercising regularly can be a terrific method to increase self-confidence and feel good about your physical appearance (Ratey, 2019).

3. Can improve mood

Exercise's impact on your general mood is yet an additional advantage for your mental health. According to an array of studies, engaging in regular physical activity is linked to an improvement in mood and a decrease in negative thoughts. So, if you're having a bad day, you might just need one workout to change your perspective and overcome minor sadness.

4. Can promote better sleep

One commonly overlooked factor in maintaining mental health is how well you sleep at night. Although several things affect how well you sleep, physical activity is particularly important.

A 2017 review of 34 studies concluded that exercise, regardless of the type, can improve sleep efficiency and duration (Ratey, 2019). Exercise may also shorten the time it takes you to fall asleep or sleep onset latency. Therefore, regular exercise — regardless of the kind — may be very beneficial if you have trouble getting enough sleep.

WORKOUT TIMELINE

So, we know that exercise can be used to manage stress, which is also recommended as a powerful tool to reset the discourse of depression. It's confusing how much time you might want to spend working out. Regular moderate to vigorous aerobic exercise for 150 minutes per week or shorter sessions can improve the body's ability to handle and recover from stress. Resistance exercise can also provide a break from stressors, although it produces different physiological adaptations compared to aerobic exercise. It can still be beneficial for stress relief and provide general health benefits with 2 to 3 days of exercise targeting major muscle groups with a moderate intensity of 8 to 12 repetitions. Now, it's confusing, so let me break it down for you— if you are not looking to commit to a workout schedule, find something you love to do that makes you sweat and slowly incorporate it into your life.

MEDITATION

Unsurprisingly, yoga and meditation have become a widespread form of releasing tension in the youth. The fitness industry emphasizes dedicating 10 minutes of your morning to doing breathing exercises or stretching your body. You can truly rely on several free youtube videos where mentors and instructors teach people how to meditate and find inner peace. But, be careful about the posture; make sure you find someone who can help you master the posture of your pose. Recently, reviews on Tai Chi and yoga suggest that performing 2 to 3 sessions per week, lasting between 60 to 90 minutes each, can help reduce stress and improve well-being (Mayo Clinic, n.d.). A worksite study found that even shorter sessions of 15 minutes involving chair-based yoga postures were effective in reducing acute stress, as determined by self-report and physiological measures such as respiration rate and heart rate variability (Mayo Clinic, n.d.). This indicates that brief sessions can also be helpful in reducing stress through this type of exercise.

Circling back to the stance on posture. It's common knowledge that an open posture and taller stance enable a person to feel more confident and comfortable in their body and with being exposed to the world. It is associated with presenting greater confidence and ease to others. Many individuals find orderliness around the firm military stance and like the statuesque poses of ballerinas and dancers (Kim, 2018). It appears that by adopting a less anxious posture when you are in front of others, you can influence how you feel internally. Working on your posture may be the first step to recovering your mental health because the body and the mind are frequently interconnected.

Peace and Calmness

The discourse of mediation is readily linked to the idea of calmness. But I want to give you a different perspective. Yoga or meditation also makes you mindful of your body and soul. Mindfulness enables people to be fully present and aware of who they are, where they are, and what they do in their lives (Jaret, 2020). Besides, it also helps ensure that we avoid being overly reactive or overwhelmed by what's happening around us.

Your mental well-being and general health can be improved by the calm, peace, and balance that meditation can bring you. Focusing on something peaceful allows you to unwind and handle stress effectively. Meditation can also help you focus and maintain inner peace.

And once your meditation session is over, these advantages continue to exist. You can go through your day more tranquil if you practice meditation. Additionally, meditation may aid in managing certain medical disorders' symptoms (Jaret, 2020). So, practicing meditation is one way to go about it when it comes to managing stress and improving your overall health (Jaret, 2020).

According to a study in the journal Psychiatry Research, patients with anxiety disorder who participated in a course in mindfulness-based stress reduction, where they learned a variety of stress management techniques, had lower levels of stress-related hormones and inflammatory substances than those who did not practice mindfulness (Jaret, 2020). It is evident from the conclusion that meditation had a positive effect on their mental well-being.

Additionally, studies show that even brief meditation sessions can help manage stress, and they can start to work very rapidly. So, get hold of your best friend, some yoga mats, and try out new poses.

The importance of meditation can be extracted from a study conducted and published in the journal Psychoneuroendocrinology, where a group of people was split into two groups: one that underwent three days straight of 25-minute sessions on mindful meditation, and the other that learned how to analyze poetry as a way to hone their critical thinking abilities (Jaret, 2020). So, if you suffer from negative thoughts, engaging in some peaceful exercise can improve your overall mood. However, there are certain elements that you need to be aware of when embarking on your meditation journey. Some of the most common features of meditation include the following:

1. Focused attention

In meditation, a key element is the ability to concentrate your mind. By directing your attention to a specific object, image, mantra, or even your breath, you can free your mind from distractions, stress, and worries (Chopra, 2022).

2. Relaxed breathing

In this technique, practice slow and even breathing to expand your lungs with the help of your diaphragm muscle. The goal is to increase oxygen intake, breathe more efficiently, and minimize the use of shoulder, neck, and upper chest muscles.

3. A quiet setting

If you're a beginner, it could be simpler to meditate in a place with few distractions. With honed meditation skills, you can practice meditation anywhere, even in high-stress situations which would benefit you the most, such as during a traffic jam or a tough work meeting.

4. A comfortable position

You can meditate whether you're seated, lying down, walking, or engaged in another activity.To maximize the benefits of your meditation, focus on being at ease. Ensure you maintain a straight spine throughout your practice (Chopra, 2022).

5. Open attitude

Let thoughts pass through your mind without judgment. Your mind is a vortex of intrusive thoughts, don't be afraid of them. Let meditation dissolve all the negative thoughts and encapsulate your soul with goodness and peace (Welch & Gillihan, 2022).

So, you must be curious about the important techniques a beginner should know when stepping into their meditation mantra. I have accumulated 6 best practices that are crucial if you want to meditate; these include:

6. Sound meditation

Sound meditation can be as simple as immersing yourself in music. However, you can do a sound meditation on your own by selecting soothing music without vocals that feel uplifting (Thomas, 2020). The goal is to allow yourself to absorb the music to create a harmonious state of mind, which can help to heal dissonance and promote positive thoughts.

7. Guided meditation

The name of the meditation is self-explanatory; in this type of meditation, you rely on apps and youtube videos to perfect your poses. Getting started with guided meditation can also be accomplished using a meditation app which even yoga instructors agree is beneficial (Thomas, 2020).

8. Kindness meditation

Loving-kindness meditation, also known as Metta meditation, is a valuable practice, particularly in the current climate. This technique involves generating compassion for ourselves and others, including the entire world. Self-compassion is the foundation for compassion towards others, and it can aid in cultivating joy, love, forgiveness, and healing (Thomas, 2020). So, it is crucial for you to indulge in self-awareness and love before embarking on this journey.

In the end, it's important for you to find ways that bring your mind peace. So, when you regain your confidence and recognize your inner strengths, you can approach every challenge that life throws at you with a clear mind. In fact, this also helps you avoid any impulsive decisions. Truly, working out or moving your body ensures that your mind is distracted from the negative thoughts that your mind ends up exploring.

UNLOCKING THE POWER OF WORDS

"Journaling helps you remember how strong you truly are within yourself."

— ASAD MEAH

Asad Meah has it all figured out, especially when it comes to journaling. This one statement of Asad signifies the importance of journaling and releasing tension using words. Journaling has a colossal impact on your mental health, as you are able to pen down every thought that comes to your mind.

IMPORTANCE OF JOURNALISM

Many people keep their journals beneath their mattresses when they are teenagers. For me, my cupboard was the safe space where I would lock away my little diary filled with intrusive thoughts. It was a safe place to share my challenges and anxieties without fear of ridicule or retaliation. Do you keep a journal? I felt relieved to put all of those emotions and ideas on paper. The world appeared more lucid and free of stress.

Keeping a diary might be an excellent option if you experience stress, despair, or anxiety. You may be able to better manage how you feel and maintain improved psychological wellness.

It's possible that after you enter maturity, you would not want to maintain a journal, but honestly, every time I go back to my journals from high school, it reminds me of how far I have come. The idea and its advantages still hold true. Simply expressing your ideas and feelings in words can help you comprehend them better. It is known as journaling in modern society and is a brilliant way to release negative thoughts.

BENEFITS OF JOURNALING

Finding a healthy outlet for your emotions when they are too much to handle is crucial, and keeping a diary may be a good method. You may cope with depression, manage stress, and control anxiety by penning down your emotions in a notebook. By prioritizing issues, fears, and concerns, keeping track of symptoms on a daily basis, allowing for constructive self-talk, and recognizing unhelpful ideas and behaviors, journaling aids in alleviating symptoms and mood improvement. It can also assist you in figuring out the root reasons for your stress and developing a strategy to deal with them. It helps you become aware of your emotions and develop fresh perspectives on occurrences when you write down how you feel about a challenging scenario.

Writing about sentiments in an abstract fashion might be more relaxing than writing realistically, according to studies showing that individuals who write regarding what they have experienced become more capable of managing their emotions. Additionally, writing in private about a tumultuous experience could inspire individuals to seek out social support; this can aid in recovering from emotional trauma. Overall, keeping a diary is an effective tool that may enhance your general well-being and assist you in managing your mental wellness.

Sustaining a healthy way of life and managing anxiety, panic attacks, and psychological disorders include many different components, including journaling. To maximize the advantages of journaling, additional crucial procedures should be followed. You may quiet your mind and lessen tension by relaxing and practicing meditation every day. A healthy, balanced diet contains the nutrients required for mental and physical wellness. To maintain a healthy body and mind, regular exercise is necessary. Additionally, essential for mental wellness is getting adequate sleep each night. Finally, you should refrain from using drugs and alcohol since they harm your emotional and psychological health.

Keep a notebook to monitor your development and ensure you adhere to these rules every day. You may enhance your general state of mind and successfully regulate anxiety, depression, stress, and mental health issues by incorporating these good behaviors into your daily routine and utilizing your notebook as a tool to hold yourself responsible.

HOW TO JOURNAL

To begin started journaling, consider using these suggestions:

1. Contingently try to write. Daily writing time should be allotted. Your journaling will improve as a result of this.
2. Simplify it. Ensure that you always have a pen and paper with you. When you're ready, you can put your ideas down.
3. Using your smartphone, you may also journal. Whenever it feels appropriate, write or sketch.
4. No particular organization is required for your journal. You may talk and make anything you want to convey your emotions in your own private space.
5. Give full rein to your thoughts and words. Neither spelling errors nor what others could believe should be a concern (Ballas, 2021).

Make any necessary use of your journal. Nobody requires you to divulge the contents of your journal. You might display portions of your notebook to close family and friends if you wish to share some of your ideas with them.

When everything seems chaotic, keeping a diary might help you bring order to your surroundings. By disclosing your most intimate anxieties, ideas, and feelings, you come to know yourself. Take into consideration the time you spend writing as personal downtime. You are able to unwind and wind down during this period. Write while sipping tea in a peaceful, tranquil environment. Enjoy the time you spend writing in your diary. Furthermore, be aware that you are also taking care of your mental and physical health.

JOURNALING AND SELF CONFIDENCE

A lack of self-esteem has been connected to problems with eating, social disengagement, and depression. 85% of Americans, according to a 2017 NBC survey, have poor self-esteem (Alton, 2017).

It is obvious that "giving everyone a trophy" has not helped improve the confidence of children, teenagers, or adults as we hear accounts of bullying during childhood and rising rates of anxiety, despair, and mortality. There are better approaches to encourage a compassionately based sense of self-worth, self-acceptance, and self-love.

Self-confidence is one of the areas of social psychology concepts that has been studied the most. Children, students, competitors, and employees are constantly being encouraged to develop their own sense of self by their parents, instructors, coaches, and mentors. It is essential to wellness, achievement, and life happiness.

The mindset a person has towards oneself, and their perception of their importance to the world is known as self-esteem. The caliber of our self-perceptions is important because we are constantly impacted by the beliefs, principles, and behaviors we hold.

SELF-LOVE JOURNAL PROMPTS

Using prompts in your diary is a terrific idea. They may offer guidance, inspiration, and diversity so the habit doesn't become routine.

To develop self-awareness, self-acceptance, and self-compassion, keep in mind that the goal of a self-esteem notebook is to promote positive introspection. Here are 7 prompts you can take inspiration from:

1. Recognize your advantages

Write down concrete instances of acts, behaviors, or accomplishments that showcase each of your top three qualities (Madeson & Nash, 2020).

2. Feel grateful

Give specifics about the top three things in your life for which you are thankful. How have they affected your body, mind, emotions, and spirit?

3. Imagine your ideal day

But try to keep it relatively grounded. Describe your actions, your surroundings, and your feelings in each case.

4. Consider a recent achievement and what it reveals about your character

Consider an accomplishment or "win" you have recently experienced. Then describe how this achievement exemplifies a strength or attribute that you have (Madeson & Nash, 2020).

5. Recognize your efforts

Success is not the only factor in self-esteem. It also acknowledges that our dedication, tenacity, commitment, and perseverance are necessary steps in developing exceptional qualities. Consider a recent obstacle you overcame and how you persevered despite the result (Madeson & Nash, 2020).

6. Think about the real individuals in your life

Consider your relationship with individuals and the significance of that relationship. You should describe both your and their effects on you in your essay.

7. Write about what makes you special

This is frequently harder than emphasizing our advantages. However, consider this and offer examples. Discuss your preferred future, including achieving goals in your journal. Describe your qualities, abilities, and resources that will help make accomplishment achievable.

At the end of the day, journaling is another form of self-care that positively impacts your self-confidence. When you can regulate your emotions and thoughts, you eventually manifest success.

CONCLUSION

Conclusively, self-confidence is "the belief in your abilities and qualities; hence it focuses on your faith in your abilities and your overall sense of worth. There are several teens and adults that struggle with low self-confidence. Now, why are self-confidence and self-esteem so important?

For starters, self-confidence allows you to take on new challenges and push yourself out of your comfort zone. It helps you trust in your abilities and make decisions with conviction. Self-confidence can also help you develop better relationships, both personal and professional, by allowing you to communicate more effectively and assertively. On the other hand, self-esteem is crucial for your mental health and well-being. When you have a positive sense of self-worth, you're more likely to have a positive outlook on life and feel better about yourself. This, in turn, can help reduce stress and anxiety, improve your relationships, and lead to a more fulfilling life. But why do people suffer from low self-confidence? As explored in the first chapter, the contributors to low self-esteem are life experiences that mainly occur during childhood and adolescence.

Similarly, Misinformation can be a significant factor in low self-confidence. For example, unrealistic beauty standards are portrayed in the media. The toxic environments people are exposed to and the unsupportive people we encounter alongside anxiety and depression. Seeking support from a mental health professional can help identify and address the underlying issues.

That said, building your self-confidence back is important if you want to excel in life. Therefore, in order to regain your confidence, there are various things that you can do, such as find hobbies to excel in, become assertive, and find your inner strengths and work on them. Interestingly, as you must have explored in chapters 3 and 8, some of us have a really loud and mean inner critic. What that voice says and how it says it has a lot to do with the things we were told growing up. Your inner critic tries to overpower the positivity that resurfaces when you are rebuilding your confidence. It eventually fuels your negative thoughts and also poisons your mind with guilt. So, in order to avoid that, you can rely on positive affirmations. Besides, it's important for you to treat your failures as examples and not something that is bad. This way, you are able to not repeat your mistakes and learn from them for the future. Also, educate yourself about the adversaries of social media. Chapter 5 gives an in-depth review of how you can help yourself when and if you find yourself surfing through the social media rabbit hole. Social media can have devastating impacts on impressionable minds. It forces young girls and even boys to constantly compare themselves, exposes them to unrealistic beauty standards, etc. It's important to have healthy restrictions when using social media as a tool and not for leisure.

Moreover, another concern when it comes to improving self-confidence is procrastination. Procrastination is essentially a failure to self-regulate, making you feel like you are not in control of yourself and eroding your confidence at its core. Low self-confidence also causes procrastination by acting as a protective mechanism. When you lack confidence, taking action on tasks becomes risky, as failure can further damage your self-esteem. Your subconscious mind tries to protect you from difficult tasks that can potentially deliver another devastating blow to your confidence. Therefore, you procrastinate because you don't want to fail or fall short of your own standards, and you put off starting the task. You can always eliminate this by distracting yourself, making a realistic to-do list, and giving yourself a reward every time you check something off the list.

Subsequently, another brilliant way to regain your confidence is indulging in self-care. Self-care allows you to take time for yourself and your mind. Promoting healthy functioning and enhancing well-being is important; self-care is a multidimensional and multifaceted process involving purposeful engagement in various strategies. Self-care refers to people's conscious efforts to improve their physical, mental, and emotional health. Good self-care can take many forms, such as getting enough sleep, taking breaks for fresh air, and indulging in enjoyable activities. So, it's essential for developing resilience towards unavoidable stressors in life. When you care for your mind and body, you become better equipped to live your best life. Unfortunately, some people consider self-care a luxury rather than a priority, resulting in feelings of overwhelm, tiredness, and inadequacy when facing life's challenges.

Lastly, journaling and exercising are two tested ways of reducing anxiety and increasing self-confidence. When you look good, you feel good. Exercise can help you manage anxiety since it diverts your attention from the cause of your worries. You can ease muscle tension, which contributes to feelings of anxiety, by exercising your body. Additionally, regular exercise can help us develop the necessary resources to withstand powerful emotions. Again, there is evidence that exercise positively affects your mental health. Moreover, engaging in peaceful exercise such as yoga can help you pursue calmness, bringing your mind at ease. Overall, you are in control of your life and thoughts, so don't be afraid to pursue your ambitions and become successful.

REFERENCES

Ackerman, C. E., & Nash, J. (2018, July 12). What Is Self-Acceptance? 25 Exercises + Definition & Quotes. Positive Psychology. Retrieved May 8, 2023, from https://positivepsychology.com/self-acceptance/#examples-self-acceptance

Ackerman, C. E., & Nash, J. (2018, July 18). *Building Strong Self-Belief: 16 Tips & Activities.* PositivePsychology.com. Retrieved April 17, 2023, from https://positivepsychology.com/self-confidence-self-belief/#examples-self-confidence

Araya, A. (2023, February 2). *5 Ways to Identify Your Strengths and What You're Good At!* Tracking Happiness. Retrieved May 8, 2023, from https://www.trackinghappiness.com/how-to-identify-your-strengths/

Bailen, N. (2018, November 29). *How to Deal with Feeling Bad About Your Feelings.* Healthline. Retrieved April 17, 2023, from https://www.healthline.com/health/deal-with-guilt-about-anxiety-depression#Dealing-with-feelings-about-feelings

Ballas, P. (2021). *Journaling for Mental Health - Health Encyclopedia - University of Rochester Medical Center.* URMC. Retrieved May 8, 2023, from https://www.urmc.rochester.edu/encyclopedia/content.aspx?ContentID=4552&ContentTypeID=1

Bariso, J. (2021, October 3). *I Was a 'Master' Procrastinator. Here's the Simple 5-Step Method I Used to Quit the Habit.* Inc. Magazine. Retrieved May 8, 2023, from https://www.inc.com/justin-bariso/i-was-a-master-procrastinator-heres-simple-5-step-method-i-used-to-quit-habit.html

Best Parental Control Apps in 2022, Tested by Our Editors - Para Meninos. (n.d). Retrieved July 31, 2023, from https://parameninos.com/best-parental-control-apps-in-2022-tested-by-our-editors.html.

Better Health. (2019). *Self esteem.* Better Health Channel. Retrieved April 1, 2023, from https://www.betterhealth.vic.gov.au/health/healthyliving/self-esteem

Boland, M. (2020, November 23). *How to Stop Feeling Guilty: 10 Tips*. Healthline. Retrieved April 17, 2023, from https://www.healthline.com/health/mental-health/how-to-stop-feeling-guilty#learn-from-the-past

Brennan, D. (2021, October 25). *How Journaling Can Help Ease Anxiety and Encourage Healing*. WebMD. Retrieved May 8, 2023, from https://www.webmd.com/mental-health/mental-health-benefits-of-journaling

Broster, A. (2021). *Home*. YouTube. Retrieved April 1, 2023, from https://www.forbes.com/sites/alicebroster/2021/01/31/girls-have-much-lower-self-esteem-during-their-teen-years-according-to-new-study/?sh=68ad7f515eb7

Brown, J. (2022, September 8). *How to Respond to a Guilt Trip*. Mindpath Health. Retrieved April 17, 2023, from https://www.mindpath.com/resource/how-to-respond-to-a-guilt-trip/

Bubnis, D., Preiato, D., & Ditzell, J. (2022, January 31). *Mental Health Benefits of Exercise: For Depression and More*. Healthline. Retrieved May 8, 2023, from https://www.healthline.com/health/depression/exercise#Exercise-and-attention-deficit-hyperactivity-disorder-(ADHD)

Cassata, C. (2019, September 3). *What Is Self-Care?* Healthline. Retrieved May 8, 2023, from https://www.healthline.com/health-news/self-care-is-not-just-treating-yourself#How-to-incorporate-self-care-habits

Chadha, K. (2021, January 19). *The Concept Of Overthinking And Procrastination.* Eat My News. Retrieved May 8, 2023, from https://www.eatmy.news/2021/01/the-concept-of-overthinking-and.html

Cherry, K. (2022, July 22). *Why Are Emotions Important?* Verywell Mind. Retrieved April 17, 2023, from https://www.verywellmind.com/the-purpose-of-emotions-2795181

Cherry, K. (2022, November 8). *Guilt Complex: Definition, Symptoms, Traits, Causes, Treatment.* Verywell Mind. Retrieved April 17, 2023, from https://www.verywellmind.com/guilt-complex-definition-symptoms-traits-causes-treatment-5115946

Cherry, K. (2022, November 14). *Procrastination: Why It Happens and How to Overcome It.* Verywell Mind. Retrieved May 8, 2023, from https://www.verywellmind.com/the-psychology-of-procrastination-2795944#citation-10

Cherry, K. (2023, February 13). *11 Signs of Low Self-Esteem.* Verywell Mind. Retrieved May 10, 2023, from https://www.verywellmind.com/signs-of-low-self-esteem-5185978

Cherry, K. (2023, March 10). *Self-Awareness: Development, Types, and How to Improve.* Verywell Mind. Retrieved May 8, 2023, from https://www.verywellmind.com/what-is-self-awareness-2795023#toc-how-to-improve-your-self-awareness

Chopra, A. (2022). *Top Health Benefits Of Meditation | SocialDhara.* Retrieved August 4, 2023, from https://socialdhara.com/top-health-benefits-of-meditation/

Crumpler, C. (2022, April 25). *Positive Affirmations for Anxiety: Reframing Your Worry to Calm Down.* Psych Central. Retrieved May 8, 2023, from https://psychcentral.com/anxiety/affirmations-for-anxiety#social-anxiety

Cuncic, A. (2020, August 9). *How to Parent Teens With Social Anxiety.* Verywell Mind. Retrieved April 17, 2023, from https://www.verywellmind.com/how-to-parent-teens-with-social-anxiety-3024398

Cusack, J. (2018, January 19). *Identifying Your Feelings.* Psychology Today. Retrieved April 17, 2023, from https://www.psychologytoday.com/us/blog/art-and-science/201801/identifying-your-feelings

Damasio, A. R. (2022). *The Science of Emotion*. Library of Congress. Retrieved April 17, 2023, from https://www.loc.gov/loc/brain/emotion/Damasio.html

Deveraux, M. (2020, February 29). *The Dangers of Social Media for Teens*. Outback Therapeutic Expeditions. Retrieved May 8, 2023, from https://www.outbacktreatment.com/the-dangers-of-social-media-for-teens/

Faithtoh. (2022). *Why Negative Emotions Aren't All Bad. Hope Channel Singapore*. Retrieved July 5, 2022, from https://hopechannel.sg/expert-advice/mind-body/why-negative-emotions-arent-all-bad/.

Galperin, S. (2022). *8 Tips for Teens with Social Anxiety - CBT Psychology*. CBT Psychology for Personal Development. Retrieved April 17, 2023, from https://cbtpsychology.com/7-tips-teens-with-social-anxiety/

Georgiou, A. (2018). *How Do Thoughts and Emotions Affect Health? | Taking Charge of Your Health & Wellbeing*. Taking Charge of Your Health & Wellbeing. Retrieved April 17, 2023, from https://www.takingcharge.csh.umn.edu/how-do-thoughts-and-emotions-affect-health

Georgiou, A. (2019). *What Are Thoughts & Emotions? | Taking Charge of Your Health & Wellbeing*. Taking Charge of Your Health & Wellbeing. Retrieved April 17, 2023, from https://www.takingcharge.csh.umn.edu/what-are-thoughts-emotions

Gepp, K. (2018, August 22). *Emotional Stress: Symptoms and Signs*. Healthline. Retrieved April 17, 2023, from https://www.healthline.com/health/emotional-symptoms-of-stress#outlook

Glicksman, E. (2019, September 12). *Your Brain on Guilt and Shame*. BrainFacts. Retrieved April 17, 2023, from https://www.brainfacts.org/thinking-sensing-and-behaving/emotions-stress-and-anxiety/2019/your-brain-on-guilt-and-shame-091219

Gordon, S. (2021, July 26). *Boundaries: What Every Teen Needs to Know*. Verywell Family. Retrieved April 17, 2023, from https://www.verywellfamily.com/boundaries-what-every-teen-needs-to-know-5119428

Goulding, C. S. (2017). *5 Ways To Get Rid Of Guilt & Move On With Your Life*. MindBodyGreen. Retrieved April 17, 2023, from https://www.mindbodygreen.com/articles/how-to-get-rid-of-guilt

Griggs, U. (2023, March 8). *How to Find Your Inner Strength and Let It Shine*. LifeHack. Retrieved May 8, 2023, from https://www.lifehack.org/841468/inner-strength#what-is-inner-strength

Hage, J. (2019). *5 Ways Overwhelmed Overthinkers Can Beat Procrastination*. Filling the Jars. Retrieved May 8, 2023, from https://www.fillingthejars.com/5-ways-overwhelmed-overthinkers-beat-procrastination/

Hui, A. (2021, September 28). *Causes of Negative Self Talk and How to Overcome It*. Olympia Benefits. Retrieved May 8, 2023, from https://www.olympiabenefits.com/blog/causes-of-negative-self-talk-and-how-to-overcome-it

Hunt, E. (2021, January 6). *Silence your inner critic: a guide to self-compassion in the toughest times*. The Guardian. Retrieved May 8, 2023, from https://www.theguardian.com/lifeandstyle/2021/jan/06/silence-your-inner-critic-a-guide-to-self-compassion-in-the-toughest-times

Jackson, E. (2022, July 29). *The Role of Exercise in Stress Management*. Retrieved May 8, 2023, from https://journals.lww.com/acsm-healthfitness/fulltext/2013/05000/stress_relief__the_role_of_exercise_in_stress.6.aspx

James, W., & Lange, C. (2019, June 27). *The Science of Emotion: Exploring the Basics of Emotional Psychology | UWA Online*. University of West Alabama Online. Retrieved April 17, 2023, from https://online.uwa.edu/news/emotional-psychology/

Jaret, P. (2020, July 8). *What is Mindfulness?* Mindful.org. Retrieved May 8, 2023, from https://www.mindful.org/what-is-mindfulness/

Johnson, J., & Duron, A. (2021, January 4). *Easy Confidence Boosters: 19 Way to Improve Self-Esteem*. Greatist. Retrieved April 1, 2023, from https://greatist.com/grow/easy-confidence-boosters

Juby, B. (2018, August 22). *The No BS Guide to Mastering Unwanted Emotions*. Healthline. Retrieved April 17, 2023, from https://www.healthline.com/health/mental-health/developing-self-awareness

Karimian, Chagin, & Sävendahl. (2012). Genetic regulation of the growth plate. Frontiers in endocrinology, 2, 113. https://doi.org/10.3389/fendo.2011.00113.

Kim, J. (2018, June 12). *Can Good Posture Help Mental Health?* Psychology Today. Retrieved May 8, 2023, from https://www.psychologytoday.com/us/blog/culture-shrink/201806/can-good-posture-help-mental-health

Kreitzer, M. J. (2019). *What Is Mindfulness? | Taking Charge of Your Health & Wellbeing*. Taking Charge of Your Health & Wellbeing. Retrieved May 9, 2023, from https://www.takingcharge.csh.umn.edu/what-mindfulness

Lawler, M., & Gillihan, S. (2023). *What Is Self-Care, and Why Is It So Important for Your Health?* Everyday Health. Retrieved April 27, 2023, from https://www.everydayhealth.com/self-care/

Lawrenz, L. (2020). *7 Tips to Manage ADHD Procrastination.* Psych Central. Retrieved May 8, 2023, from https://psychcentral.com/adhd/how-to-stop-adhd-procrastination#recap

Legg, T. J. (n.d.). *How to Stop Ruminating: 10 Tips to Stop Repetitive Thoughts.* Healthline. Retrieved April 13, 2023, from https://www.healthline.com/health/how-to-stop-ruminating

Litner, J. (2020, April 28). *How to Control Your Emotions: 11 Strategies to Try.* Healthline. Retrieved April 17, 2023, from https://www.healthline.com/health/how-to-control-your-emotions#get-some-space

Madeson, M., & Nash, J. (2020, June 14). *Self-Esteem Journals, Prompts, PDFs and Ideas.* Positive Psychology. Retrieved May 8, 2023, from https://positivepsychology.com/self-esteem-journal-prompts/

Markway, B., & Ampel, C. (2018, December 7). *5 Reasons People Have Low Self-Confidence.* Psychology Today. Retrieved May 10, 2023, from https://www.psychologytoday.com/us/blog/shyness-is-nice/201812/5-reasons-people-have-low-self-confidence

Mathew, S. (2022, May 14). *How to Be Responsible Using Social Media as a Student.* CollegeXpress. Retrieved May 8, 2023, from https://www.collegexpress.com/articles-and-advice/student-life/blog/how-to-be-responsible-using-social-media-as-a-student/

Mayo Clinic. (n.d.). *Meditation: Take a stress-reduction break wherever you are.* Mayo Clinic. Retrieved May 8, 2023, from https://www.mayoclinic.org/tests-procedures/meditation/in-depth/meditation/art-20045858

Mayo Clinic. (2019). *Positive thinking: Reduce stress by eliminating negative self-talk.* Mayo Clinic. Retrieved May 8, 2023, from https://www.mayoclinic.org/healthy-lifestyle/stress-management/in-depth/positive-thinking/art-20043950

Mayo Clinic Staff. (2018). *Teens and social media use: What's the impact?* Mayo Clinic. Retrieved May 8, 2023, from https://www.mayoclinic.org/healthy-lifestyle/tween-and-teen-health/in-depth/teens-and-social-media-use/art-20474437

Mead, E., & Smith, W. (2019, April 8). *What are Negative Emotions and How to Control Them?* PositivePsychology.com. Retrieved April 17, 2023, from https://positivepsychology.com/negative-emotions/

Morin, A. (2021, February 20). *8 Self-Esteem Builders for Teens: How to Boost Your Teen's Confidence.* Verywell

Family. Retrieved April 1, 2023, from https://www.verywellfamily.com/essential-strategies-for-raising-a-confident-teen-2611002

Morin, A. (2021, September 1). *Ask a Therapist: How Can I Improve My Self-Esteem?* Verywell Mind. Retrieved April 17, 2023, from https://www.verywellmind.com/ask-a-therapist-how-can-i-improve-my-self-esteem-5095001

Morin, A. (2022, February 23). (⎯ ⎯ ;). YouTube. Retrieved May 8, 2023, from https://www.forbes.com/sites/amymorin/2014/11/06/taming-your-inner-critic-7-steps-to-silencing-the-negativity/?sh=935e23c7feb7

NewFolks. (2022, July 22). *6 Ways Teens Can Use Social Media to Boost Self-Esteem*. NewFolks. Retrieved May 8, 2023, from https://www.newfolks.com/stages/teens-social-media-self-esteem/#dt-heading-entrepreneurial-inspiration-gained-through-social-media

9 ways to cultivate inner strength and resilience. (n.d.). Tony Robbins. Retrieved May 8, 2023, from https://www.tonyrobbins.com/business/inner-strength/

Pew Research Center. (2022, August 10). *Teens, Social Media and Technology 2022.* Pew Research Center. Retrieved May 8, 2023, from https://www.pewre

search.org/internet/2022/08/10/teens-social-media-and-technology-2022/

Pflug, T. (2022, October 25). *How To Deal With Your Emotions & Boost Your Self-Confidence*. Personal Development Zone. Retrieved April 17, 2023, from https://personal-development-zone.com/emotions-and-self-confidence/

Pope, K. R. (2019). *How Self-Confident Are You? - Improving Self-Confidence by Building Self-Efficacy*. Mind Tools. Retrieved March 31, 2023, from https://www.mindtools.com/ahqz3nl/how-self-confident-are-you

Positive Self Talk: What It Is and Why It's Important? - Conflict Center. (n.d.). The Conflict Center. Retrieved May 8, 2023, from https://conflictcenter.org/positive-self-talk-what-it-is-and-why-its-important/

Psych Central. (2021, June 21). *Tips to Soothe Your Worries of What Others Think of You*. Psych Central. Retrieved May 1, 2023, from https://psychcentral.com/blog/mental-shifts-to-stop-caring-what-people-think-of-you#tips

Quenqua, D. (2012, November 19). *Teenage Boys, Worried About Body Image, Take Health Risks*. The New York Times. Retrieved April 1, 2023, from https://www.nytimes.com/2012/11/19/health/teenage-boys-worried-about-body-image-take-risks.html?pagewanted=all&_r=0.

Radically Improve Your Self-Confidence with These Top 10 Self-Care Ideas. (n.d.). Lake Louise Wellness. Retrieved May 8, 2023, from https://www.lakelouisewellness.com/single-post/self-care-ideas-for-self-confidence

Ratey, J. J. (2019, October 24). *Can exercise help treat anxiety?* Harvard Health. Retrieved May 8, 2023, from https://www.health.harvard.edu/blog/can-exercise-help-treat-anxiety-2019102418096

Raypole, C. (2019). *List of Emotions: 53 Ways to Express What You're Feeling.* Healthline. Retrieved August 2, 2023, from https://www.healthline.com/health/list-of-emotions.

ReachOut. (2017). *Self-esteem and teenagers.* ReachOut Parents. Retrieved April 17, 2023, from https://parents.au.reachout.com/common-concerns/everyday-issues/self-esteem-and-teenagers

Real Research. (2022, August 18). *Over 38% Say Teenagers Spend More Than 8 Hours on Social Media Daily.* Real Research. Retrieved May 8, 2023, from https://realresearcher.com/media/over-38-percent-say-teenagers-spend-more-than-8-hours-on-social-media-daily/

Rebecca. (2019). *10 Ways To Find Your Inner Strength - Minimalism Made Simple*. Minimalism Made Simple -. Retrieved May 8, 2023, from https://www.minimalismmadesimple.com/home/inner-strength/

Rizvi, A., Russell, J., & Koch, E. (2021, July 14). *The Effects of Guilt on My Body and Mind*. Muscular Dystrophy News. Retrieved April 17, 2023, from https://musculardystrophynews.com/columns/guilt-effects-body-mind/

Rjoachim, (2023). "How to STOP Negative Self-Talk | Jim Kwik." Nutritional Direct. Retrieved July 24, 2023, from https://nutritionaldirect.com/how-to-stop-negative-self-talk-jim-kwik/

Roberts, E. (2015, March 5). *Learn How to Control Your Emotions and Feel Confident*. HealthyPlace. Retrieved April 17, 2023, from https://www.healthyplace.com/blogs/buildingselfesteem/2015/03/learn-how-to-control-your-emotions-and-feel-confident

Russell, L. (2019). *Social Anxiety in Teenagers: How to Help Your Child*. They Are The Future. Retrieved April 17, 2023, from https://www.theyarethefuture.co.uk/social-anxiety-in-teenager/

Schwarz, N. (2022, September 6). *How to Teach Growth Mindset to Teens*. Big Life Journal. Retrieved May 8,

2023, from https://biglifejournal.com/blogs/blog/teaching-teens-growth-mindset

Scott, E. (2022, February 16). *How Negative Emotions Affect Us and How to Embrace Them.* Verywell Mind. Retrieved April 17, 2023, from https://www.verywellmind.com/embrace-negative-emotions-4158317#toc-how-do-negative-emotions-affect-us

Scott, E. (2022, May 24). *How to Use Positive Self Talk for Stress Relief.* Verywell Mind. Retrieved May 8, 2023, from https://www.verywellmind.com/how-to-use-positive-self-talk-for-stress-relief-3144816

Scott, E. (2022, May 24). *The Toxic Effects of Negative Self-Talk.* Verywell Mind. Retrieved May 8, 2023, from https://www.verywellmind.com/negative-self-talk-and-how-it-affects-us-4161304

Scott, E. (2023, February 13). *5 Self-Care Practices for Every Area of Your Life.* Verywell Mind. Retrieved May 8, 2023, from https://www.verywellmind.com/self-care-strategies-overall-stress-reduction-3144729

7 Medically-Backed Ways To Prevent Addiction In Social Media Users – Medical Device News Magazine. (2022, July 23). Medical Device News Magazine. Retrieved April 18, 2023, from https://infomeddnews.com/7-medically-backed-ways-to-prevent-addiction-in-social-media-users/

Shatz, I. (2020). *Procrastination Dangers: The Negative Effects of Procrastination – Solving Procrastination.* Solving Procrastination. Retrieved May 8, 2023, from https://solvingprocrastination.com/procrastination-dangers/

Skurat, K. (2022, May 8). *What Causes Feelings of Guilt and What to Do About It.* Calmerry. Retrieved April 17, 2023, from https://us.calmerry.com/blog/self-esteem/why-do-i-feel-guilty-for-no-reason/

Taylor, E. (2018, November 14). *7 Habits You Don't Realize Can Cause Your Negative Self-Talk.* Bustle. Retrieved May 8, 2023, from https://www.bustle.com/p/7-habits-you-dont-realize-can-cause-your-negative-self-talk-13137479

Thomas, S. S. (2020, May 25). *7 Meditation Techniques for Beginners.* Allure. Retrieved May 8, 2023, from https://www.allure.com/story/beginner-meditation-techniques-tricks

Touronis, V. (2020, March 6). *Why do I feel guilty for no reason?* My Online Therapy. Retrieved April 17, 2023, from https://myonlinetherapy.com/why-do-i-feel-guilty-for-no-reason/

Tye, K., & Authors, G. (2016, April 21). *3 Causes of Low Self-Esteem in Teens (And What to Do About It).* Stop Medicine Abuse. Retrieved May 10, 2023, from https://

stopmedicineabuse.org/blog/details/3-causes-of-low-self-esteem-in-teens-and-what-to-do-about-it/

Universal Emotions | What are Emotions? (n.d.). Paul Ekman Group. Retrieved April 17, 2023, from https://www.paulekman.com/universal-emotions/

Waters, S. (2021, August 5). *The Path to Self-Acceptance.* BetterUp. Retrieved May 8, 2023, from https://www.betterup.com/blog/self-acceptance

Weissberger, T. (2019). *The Difference Between Self Confidence and Self Esteem.* Attention Deficit Disorder Association. Retrieved May 10, 2023, from https://add.org/self-confidence-vs-self-esteem/

Welch, A., & Gillihan, S. (2022, August 6). *How Meditation Can Improve Your Mental Health.* Everyday Health. Retrieved May 8, 2023, from https://www.everydayhealth.com/meditation/how-meditation-can-improve-your-mental-health/

Wilkes, J. (2022). *Self Care And Don't Forget The Water | Fontis Water.* Retrieved August 1, 2023, from https://fontiswater.com/self-care-and-dont-forget-the-water/

Wilson, D. R., & Felman, A. (2020, July 20). *Take Care of Yourself: 25 Science-Backed Self-Care Tips.* Greatist. Retrieved May 8, 2023, from https://greatist.com/

happiness/ways-to-practice-self-care#Your-action-plan

Winwood, M. (2019). *What Causes Guilt & How To Overcome It.* AXA Health. Retrieved April 17, 2023, from https://www.axahealth.co.uk/health-information/mental-health/resilience/what-causes-guilt-and-how-to-overcome-it/

Printed in Great Britain
by Amazon